Ancient Civilizations

TIME LIFE Student Library

3000 BC — AD 500

Ancient Civilizations

Time-Life Books   Alexandria, Virginia

Table of Contents

Early Humans

For hundreds of thousands of years our **ancestors** lived like the people in the painting at right. **Archaeologists** have gathered information about what life was like so long ago from fossilized bones and stone tools. The oldest of these **artifacts** were found in East Africa.

AFRICA

Olduvai Gorge

ATLANTIC OCEAN

INDIAN OCEAN

It was a harsh and uncertain existence for these early humans; they probably moved from place to place in small groups of families while searching for wild plants and hunting for animals to eat. They had to compete with much bigger, stronger predators for food, fighting off the ancestors of today's lions, leopards, and hyenas. From the scattered bones left lying around ancient campfires, scholars have learned that these people ate hippopotamus, antelope, buffalo, and elephant.

To avoid becoming the prey themselves, they built their camps on steep hillsides or rock outcroppings. For protection they surrounded their camps with barriers made of thorny acacia plants. In camp much of their time was devoted to making and repairing tools: sharp-edged stones, sticks, horns, and antlers. With these tools they cut meat away from carcasses, dug up edible roots, stripped bark to use as rope, and cut tree branches to build shelters.

While on the move from one camp to another, they carried food supplies in hide sacks or tied them into bundles with strips of hide or vines. They may also have carried fire, lighting torches from brush fires started by lightning strikes. About 500,000 years ago they learned how to make fire with dry sticks and dry leaves or bark. We don't know if they wore any clothing in the warm African climate, but later people began using skins to keep warm as they moved into Asia and Europe.

Then & NOW!

Stone Age Hunters

Four thousand years ago, an artist painted the graceful hunter and his prey *(left)* on a rockface in Algeria. Below, a present-day !Kung (the ! represents a clicking sound) bowman in Botswana still lives the same way. The !Kung spend about four hours each day hunting game or gathering roots and nuts for food, and use the rest of the time to talk, play games, and sleep. They know all the natural sources of food and water in their semi-desert environment.

First Tools

Simple Choppers

The earliest tools humans used were simple stone choppers. Archaeologists dug them up in the Olduvai Gorge in Tanzania, where many human **fossils** have been found. Choppers like these are about two million years old. The tool-maker struck a fist-size stone with another stone, chipping off pieces until the round stone had a sharp edge. Choppers could cut meat and shape wood. The pieces that were chipped off became scrapers and knives.

Shaped Points

Later toolmakers discovered that bone hammers were more efficient for flaking pieces off stones. They chipped all sides of the stone, making blades and points. These tools were specialized; different shapes served for cutting branches, slicing meat, or scraping skins. Some have been found grouped together, like an early tool kit.

The Great Migration

About 100,000 years ago, modern humans—**Homo sapiens sapiens**—left traces of their lives in caves near Haifa, Israel. Their skeletons and tools are the earliest evidence of today's human population living outside Africa. These hunter-gatherers followed herds of grazing animals across the **Middle East**, moving slowly, perhaps a few miles in every **generation.** Later, as the **Ice Age** glaciers retreated in the north and the climate grew milder, they wandered into Europe. They carried fire from campsite to campsite and found shelter in caves. These trailblazers discovered strange new animals. By observing what animals would eat, they found species of edible plants. Over the course of generations, they adapted to their surroundings by developing body types that were different from their African **ancestors'.**

Europe

About 40,000 years ago, modern humans first **migrated** into Europe from the Middle East. Accomplished artists, these people left jewelry, carvings, and thousands of paintings behind, like the woolly mammoth *(left)* from a cave wall in Pech Merle, France. These images give us a glimpse of their world.

Russia

Europe

France   **Ukraine**

Israel

Africa

Would You Believe?

Invention of String

String is a common household item that we take for granted today. Yet 20,000 years ago its invention produced a revolutionary change. By twisting separate plant fibers together to make long string, people had the means to tame their environment. They could make fishing line, nets for trapping animals, ropes, bridles, baskets, and bead necklaces. In time, people learned to weave lengths of string into cloth.

Ukraine

As people moved farther east, about 18,000 years ago, they began to frame their shelters with bones of the woolly mammoths they hunted for food. At a site in Mezhirichi, Ukraine *(left)*, 95 mammoth jawbones were placed upright to form a wall around a shallow pit. Hides, bark, earth, and grasses covered the walls.

North America

Australia

These signature hands were painted on a rockface in Kakadu National Park, Australia, about 40,000 years ago. As early as 50,000 years ago, people crossed a 60-mile-wide strait from **Melanesia** to the vast uninhabited continent of Australia. Fishing boats blown off course by storms might have found the new land accidentally. Later, large rafts may have carried settlers there.

Australia

The Americas

Christopher Columbus didn't discover America: Ice Age peoples did! Between 25,000 and 16,000 years ago, low sea levels exposed a wide land bridge between Siberia and Alaska. Hunter-gatherer families wandered across this land bridge, following drifting animal herds. It may have taken them many years to cross, but eventually they established settlements in North and South America.

First Villages

Çatal Hüyük

When hunting bands began constructing stockades to catch wild sheep or goats alive, they became the first ranchers. They eventually built pens for keeping animals for their meat and hides. Soon they were able to **domesticate** goats, sheep, and cattle. People would visit river valleys to gather grain where it grew thick and in time learned to collect the seeds and scatter them in places of their own choosing. Farming led to more predictable food supplies; there was sometimes even a surplus. With plenty of food available, people began to stay in one place to tend their crops and animals. Larger groups built permanent homes, creating the first villages. Living together in one place allowed people to develop more complex social customs and rituals.

TURKEY

Çatal Hüyük

Mediterranean Sea

Taurus Mts.

Tigris R.

Euphrates R.

Villages formed wherever people could raise bountiful crops. In the best places the villages grew into cities. An archaeological site called Çatal Hüyük in modern Turkey contains the earliest city ever found. About 9,000 years ago the 6,000 residents herded cattle and planted lentils, peas, wheat, and barley in **irrigated** fields. They also knew how to make pottery, weave cloth, and smelt ore into metals for tools.

Çatal Hüyük was built of stacked mud-brick houses. There were no outside doorways; people climbed ladders to rooftop openings. Pulling up the ladder gave protection from attack. The living rooms were used for religious ceremonies and had shrines; the one below is decorated with bull's-head sculptures. Plaster platforms covered graves where the dead were buried with jewels or weapons.

How do we Know?

of a find is tracing the style of a piece of pottery, or the kind of paint used to decorate it, to another site whose age is known. Among the new scientific methods are **radiocarbon dating** and **thermoluminescence dating**.

How Old Is It?

Geologist Mulugeta Feseha (*right*) removes a piece of rock and checks its direction with a **compass** to record its north-south orientation. Such careful **analysis** of a layer of rock helps in dating **artifacts.** Another method to determine the age

Town of Çatal Hüyük

Fancy Pottery

Earlier, **nomadic** peoples had crafted small figurines out of clay, but they did not make pottery vessels, which would have been too heavy and fragile for a group on the move. Settled farmers, however, needed storage containers to protect seed supplies from rats and birds. The first examples of pottery—plain clay jars with rounded, uneven shapes—are about 9,000 years old. Over the next several thousand years, pottery evolved into an art form. **Artisans** decorated pots with painted scenes, colorful geometric designs, or patterns etched into the clay.

Sumer The First Civilization

About 5,000 years ago, when most people were still wandering the earth in search of food, something radically new was happening along the Tigris and Euphrates Rivers. In this region, called Mesopotamia by the ancient Greeks for "land between the rivers," in what is now part of modern-day Iraq, the world's first **civilization** evolved. The people called their land Sumer.

But why here? What gave Sumer a head start over other parts of the world? The answer lies in the land and the inventiveness of the Sumerians. The land is hot and dry, but the soil is fertile thanks to periodic flooding. Sumerian farmers devised a system of canals that turned sunbaked mud flats into lush green fields. With **irrigation,** one farmer could grow enough food to feed several families. And with a plentiful supply of food, people could turn their attention to other things. They built large walled cities, organized a government, and developed new skills and tools.

What's a Civilization?

Certain characteristics in a settled group of people make up a civilization. They are:

- a surplus of food
- a division of labor
- an organized government
- an organized religion
- a class system
- a written language
- a system of laws
- education for the young
- public works
- technology

The people of Sumer were the first to excel in all of these, as shown in some of the examples at right.

Government

Gudea, ruler of the city of Lagash, is holding a cup from which two rivers flow—an apt symbol for the country that was founded between two rivers. Each city was governed by its own king. The people believed that their kings had been chosen by the gods.

City Planning

The first towns grew without any particular order from smaller settlements, but as Sumer developed further, its cities began to show more careful planning. This clay map from 1300 BC accurately depicts the layout of the city of Nippur. A large temple is in the top right-hand corner, and a canal cuts through the city from north to southeast. The Euphrates River runs down the left side.

The First Accountants

As Sumerian **city-states** began to trade with one another, they soon realized the need for a system to keep track of goods. Their solution was the bulla—a hollow clay ball—and tokens *(right)*. To record a trade, merchants would press tokens, each representing a specific quantity of goods like a sack of grain or a jug of oil, into the bulla's soft surface. Then they would place the tokens inside the bulla and seal it. In case of dispute, the bulla could be opened and the tokens counted. Gradually this system became more sophisticated and led to the development of math and writing.

A Code of Law

In the **stele** at left King Hammurabi is given a code of law by the god Shamash, **patron** of justice. On the 4,000-year-old stone some of the earliest laws are inscribed, listing crimes and penalties. In many cases the punishment was an eye for an eye and a tooth for a tooth. For example: "If a builder constructed a house for a man, but did not make his work strong, with the result that the house which he built collapsed and so has caused the death of the owner of the house, that builder shall be put to death."

Division of Labor

The figures below show a few of the many professions found in Sumerian society, such as trader, rancher, wheat farmer, and fisherman. Because some people were freed from the burden of producing their own food, they could develop skills and knowledge never before seen. A metalsmith could produce plows for a farmer and receive grain to feed his family in return. A weaver might agree to teach his craft to the metalsmith's child in exchange for well-crafted tools. Today, money has largely replaced this kind of exchange, called barter.

Life in the City

What were Sumerian cities like? The walled cities housed as many as 50,000 people. Most families lived in mud-brick homes built on narrow, winding streets. They shopped at open-air markets for onions, beans, cucumbers, dates, apples, and cheese. Locally made items, such as pottery and clothing, as well as imported luxury goods like ivory combs or carnelian (a reddish gemstone) beads could also be purchased. In the public square people gathered to watch wrestling matches and games of chance.

There was also a downside to life. Sumerians lived in constant fear of attack from other **city-states.** Streets were unpaved, and sanitation in the crowded cities was lacking. Perhaps worst of all, there was no sewage or garbage disposal system; all refuse was simply flung into the street.

Sumerian Inventions

Sumer was the birthplace of many important technological breakthroughs, such as **irrigation,** multistory houses, and the metal plowshare. But perhaps the Sumerians' greatest invention was the wheeled vehicle.

At left is a drawing of an **archetypal** wheel based on examples found in the Sumerian cities of Susa and Kush. It consisted of three pieces of wood held together by metal ties and rimmed with copper studs. It took another thousand years before the spoked wheel was invented.

What did Sumerians look like?

Most Sumerians seem to have had one trait in common—black hair. Women styled their tresses in many ways, two of which are shown at left. The woman at top wears a pleated linen turban that conceals all of her hair except for a thin band framing her face. The woman below has her hair flowing freely down her back, with only a ribbon circling her head.

Clothing was a little less diverse. During the early days of Sumer, both men and women wore knee- to calf-length linen or wool skirts. Later, a long, shawl-like garment appeared, draped over one shoulder.

The Transportation Revolution

About 5,000 years ago a Sumerian craftsman built the first known wheeled vehicle. This was a huge advancement in transportation because an animal pulling a cart could haul two to three times as much weight as it could on its back.

Wheels also proved invaluable in case of war. The first wheeled carts, **ancestors** of the later chariot, were primitive and difficult to steer, but Sumerian armies made good use of them. Troops in wooden battle wagons, like the one above, probably went into battle ahead of the foot soldiers.

Cool Living

A typical Sumerian one- or two-story house was made of **kiln**-baked and sun-dried brick. Walls as much as 1.8 m (6 ft.) thick insulated the dwelling from the intense heat of the sun. At the center of the house was an open courtyard. The ground floor held the kitchen and the storeroom, and usually a reception room for guests. Living quarters were on the second floor under a flat roof. Ladders gave access to the roof, where the family slept on hot summer nights.

Cutaway view of a two-story house.

Water Highways

A modern fishing boat *(right)* drifts across the reed-lined Euphrates River, in Iraq, in a scene that has changed little in thousands of years. The life-giving rivers that nurtured the crops also served as the main roads through the flat, marshy landscape of Sumer. River traders and seafarers kept the city-states in contact with one another and traveled to more distant lands. Sailing as far as India and Africa, merchants traded grain and wool for stone and metal. They also brought home luxuries such as ivory, pearls, and malachite.

Lacking lumber, they bound marsh reeds together in bundles to look like logs. They built boats with these bundles, tying the ends together into a high prow and stern, similar to the seal imprint at right. Larger boats were built to the same design and proved as sea-worthy as solid wooden boats.

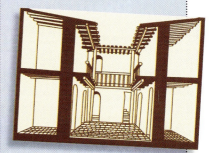

Seal Model

A boatman's seal pressed into clay *(left)* served as his signature and announced his profession. Few people could write, so most carried such seals.

Temples to Heaven

Since the Sumerians were the first people to leave written records, theirs is the oldest religion we know about. Their list of gods was long. Every natural **phenomenon** represented a god. At the top were the three creators: An of the heavens, Enlil of the air, and Enki of the waters. Besides these, every city and individual had its own **patron** god or goddess. A few of the gods are shown at right.

The temple was the center of community life in Sumer. The priests not only served the gods but also were city administrators. They collected and dispensed food, kept tax records, and oversaw the construction and maintenance of the **irrigation** canals.

The Garden of Eden?

A Sumerian myth that is similar to the story of Adam and Eve tells of the beginning of the world. The myth describes a pure and bright land that knows neither sickness nor death, where a lush garden grows. In one section of the story the god Enki is sentenced to die for eating a sacred plant. He is later reprieved and healed by eight deities, one of which bears the name Ninti, which means both "the lady of the rib" and "the lady who makes life." Elsewhere in the story Enki orders his mother to form men from "the clay that is over the abyss."

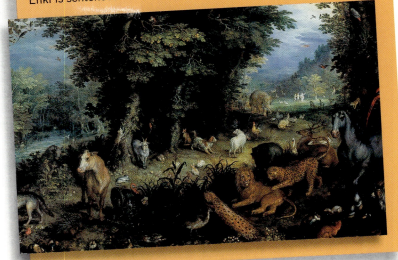

Humbaba

The Sumerians feared the fire-breathing demon Humbaba, for he caused flood, fire, and pestilence.

Nanna

In this stone carving, Nanna, the god of the moon, sits before a worshipful King Ur-Nammu. The king pours an offering to the patron god of the city of Ur. The offering may be wine, water, oil, or the blood of a newly **sacrificed** animal.

Mother Goddesses

The mother goddess Bau, shown here, always had a goose by her side. Other mother goddesses included Ninhursag, who was the highest-ranking one, and Inanna, later known as Ishtar, who controlled love, fertility, and war.

Man-Made Mountains for the Gods

Sumerians believed that the gods lived on the mountain-tops, so they built temples, called **ziggurats**, that rose to the heavens like mountains. The best-preserved example is the 4,000-year-old ziggurat at Ur *(left)*. The reconstruction above shows an additional level with a shrine on top. The base alone was 2.5 m (8 ft.) high and 45 by 60 m (150 by 200 ft.) across. A triple staircase led to the first of the three levels.

Would You Believe?

Prayer by Stand-In

The Sumerians believed that to live a long and prosperous life, they needed to appeal often to the gods. But since they couldn't spend all day praying, they made stand-ins out of stone and clay. They placed these statues in front of the altar in a position of permanent prayer. With hands clasped reverently and eyes gazing intently, the statues seemed to call to the gods on behalf of the people who had placed them there.

The Power of Writing

Without question, one of Sumer's greatest contributions to **civilization** was the written word. The earliest known examples, from about 3100 BC, are simple marks on small clay shipping tags attached to produce. At first, written symbols were artistic interpretations, or **pictographs,** of the things they represented. They were inscribed in vertical columns beginning in the right-hand corner of the **tablet.**

But sometime after 3000 BC, Sumerians switched to horizontal rows, read from left to right, just as we do today. This allowed them to write more quickly and to avoid smudging the text. Turned on their sides, the symbols looked less like pictures, and they became more **abstract.** In time the symbols evolved into a complex script of more than 700 different signs. It took years of study to learn the script, so only a small, elite portion of society, known as **scribes,** could read and write.

From Pictographs to Symbols

Sumerians first wrote in pictures on tablets and made deep impressions to represent quantities *(above)*. Later they combined signs to represent complicated ideas: A mouth and water became the verb "to drink," and a mouth and food meant "to eat." The symbols changed over time.

	3100 BC	2800 BC	2400 BC	1800 BC
Water				
To Drink				
Food				
To Eat				

What's in a Name?

Cuneiform

Sumerians didn't have pencils or pens or even paper. They used a blunt-tipped tool to write on wet clay with a series of quick, wedge-shaped impressions *(right)*. Their method became known as "cuneiform," from the **Latin** word meaning "wedge-shaped."

How do we Know?

Decoding Cuneiform

The key to translating ancient Sumerian came from these inscriptions carved on a cliff in neighboring Behistun, Iran, in 520 BC. In the **relief** Persian king Darius I *(third from the right)* judges 10 rebel chiefs. More than 1,200 lines of text list the king's achievements in three languages: Old Persian (the king's native language), Akkadian (the later form of Sumerian), and Elamite (spoken in western Persia). British linguist Sir Henry Rawlinson risked his life climbing the cliff to copy the texts placed nearly 100 m (300 ft.) above the ground. Scholars translated the Old Persian and eventually figured out the most ancient text.

School Days

Those lucky few admitted to school were assured a good job at the end of the long period of study. Students spent all year in class except for six days a month. The teaching was monotonous and the discipline harsh. One student wrote of being caned at least nine times in one day for offenses ranging from talking without permission to loitering in the street: "The fellow in charge of Sumerian said: 'Why didn't you speak Sumerian?' [He] caned me. My teacher said: 'Your hand [writing] is unsatisfactory.' [He] caned me. I [began to] hate the scribal art. . . ."

Geometry Textbooks

A fragment of a 3,800-year-old clay tablet *(top)* shows a collection of geometry exercises. Students were asked to calculate the areas of various subdivisions of squares. This was useful knowledge in a society where farmlands were laid out in long rectangular strips of different sizes. A similar, three-dimensional exercise appears in the modern-day geometry text below it.

In addition to math, pupils studied literature, medicine, law, and history. The most important subject, however, was language. Students had to master every intricacy of written Sumerian—no small task, because there were hundreds of cuneiform signs and thousands of words and phrases.

Tombs and Treasures

A royal burial was both a dazzling and a gruesome event. Because the Sumerians believed that the dead king or queen would live again in an afterlife, they filled the grave with splendid works of art and riches. In addition, dozens of servants were buried alive with the royal body to serve him or her in the next world.

The most spectacular of the graves that were discovered are from the city of Ur, one of the important **city-states** in Sumer. About 16 royal tombs have been **excavated** at Ur, but only two of them had not been plundered long ago by ancient graverobbers. Even so, the tombs contained valuable insights into the burial ceremony and into Sumerian culture in general.

The First Superhero

recovered from a tomb at Ur. The pictures illustrate the story of Gilgamesh, written in 2000 BC and the world's first **epic,** or long poem about a hero.

Gilgamesh and his friend Enkidu slew a monster with the head of a lion and the teeth of a dragon. Together they defeated the Bull of Heaven. But the gods decided Enkidu must die for murdering a heavenly beast. Gilgamesh wandered grief-stricken through the desert, fearing his own death. But he came to accept that all people must die and returned to his city a wise and good king.

Gilgamesh, the semidivine king of Uruk, wrestles two bulls in the picture above, one of several scenes that decorate the side of a bull's-head **lyre** (right)

Bull's-Head Lyre (detail)

Artifacts from the Death Pits

Warrior's Helmet

This beautiful helmet was hammered from a single sheet of gold to fit the contours of a man's head, including his ears and his long hair, which was rolled into a bun. The helmet was found in the grave of a man named Meskalamdug.

Royal Chalice

From the grave of Queen Puabi comes this 4,500-year-old gold cup. She was accompanied into the after-life by 23 servants, one of whom still had her hands on a lyre's strings.

Wreath of Gold

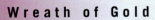

This splendid golden headdress and large hoop earrings were part of Queen Puabi's burial ensemble. The tomb held many treasures that would allow her to continue her glamorous life in the next world. In addition to her jewelry, she had on hand a supply of makeup: **stibnite** to darken her eyebrows, a purplish blue powder for her eyelids, tweezers, and a tiny earwax spoon.

British **archaeologist** Sir Leonard Woolley, pictured above removing dirt from a votive figurine, excavated the royal tombs at Ur between 1922 and 1934. Woolley believed the ruined city was the biblical "Ur of the Chaldees," described in the Book of Genesis as the birth-place of Abraham. His patience and careful work while excavating the ruins saved many priceless items, including some that were so **decayed** and fragile they could be removed only after being encased in wax.

Tales from the Tomb

An engraving from the *London Illustrated News* in 1928 shows what a scene in a death pit must have looked like. After the death of the king, more than 50 of his attendants followed him into the 10-m (33-ft.)-deep pit and took their places in front of the burial chamber. They were probably drugged and may have thought they would go to a better world. They each drank from a cup of poison and sank to the floor. Then the animals were killed, and the entrance to the grave was covered up.

An Empire's Lost Splendor

What happened to Sumer? By about 2000 BC, the region's power and wealth were waning. The fields upon which the cities' economies depended had grown less fertile through overuse. The Euphrates River had also shifted its course, leaving some riverside cities high and dry and vulnerable to outside attacks. Sumer was vanquished by a succession of foreign powers during the next 15 **centuries,** only occasionally reasserting its independence.

The first of these conquerors, the mighty Sargon of Akkad, came from the north. He consolidated the Sumerian cities under his rule to become history's first emperor. Years later, the country was incorporated into other, much larger **empires,** including Babylonia and Assyria, spreading farther north and west to the Mediterranean. In 539 BC the land became part of the Persian empire and never regained its **autonomy.**

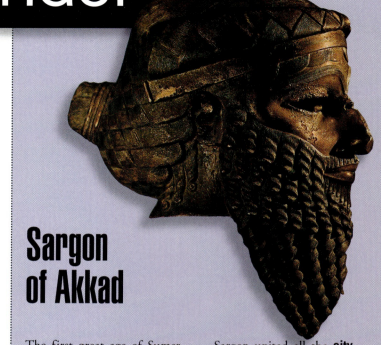

Sargon of Akkad

The first great age of Sumer came to an end in about 2300 BC when Sargon of Akkad, believed to be depicted in this bronze sculpture, invaded and took control of Sumer.

Sargon united all the **city-states** with his homeland north of Sumer. His empire reached far, but it lasted only a century or two. A revival of Sumerian **civilization** followed.

The Assyrian Empire

Imagine That!

The fierce battle shown at right demonstrates the superior military strategies for which the Assyrians were known. Three attackers scale fortifications with a ladder, while others, protecting themselves with their shields, try to breach the city's mud-brick walls with iron picks. Though outnumbered, the Assyrians prevail over their enemies, who tumble over the ramparts and drown in the river below.

The Gate of Ishtar

Dedicated to the goddess Ishtar, the majestic entryway to the city of Babylon was built at the height of the fabled city's power. Here you see the actual gate, which is now in a museum.

On the gate's blue walls rows of bulls, representing the weather god Adad, alternate with scaly-coated dragons, symbolizing Marduk, the **patron** deity of Babylon. The inset photo shows the half-mile-long main approach to the gate of the city.

The Tower of Babel

Some scholars think that Babylon's **ziggurat,** shown here as a French artist imagined it in the Middle Ages, inspired the biblical story of the Tower of Babel.

7 Wonders of the World

The Hanging Gardens

Celebrated as one of the **Seven Wonders of the World,** Babylon's Hanging Gardens were said to be built for King Nebuchadnezzar's wife, who missed her tree-filled homeland.

Egypt Land of the Pharaohs

Long before the **pharaohs** built the first pyramids in ancient Egypt, the fertile valley of the Nile River had attracted settlers. Annual floods enriched the soil and produced a surplus of grain. This abundance led to the rise of a new **civilization** there that was to last for 3,000 years.

It began about 3000 BC when a conqueror united different regions of the river valley into one country. The early Egyptians divided their world into Upper Egypt, where the river descended over waterfalls from its source in the heart of Africa, and Lower Egypt, where the river spread out to flow into the Mediterranean Sea.

We know a lot about these early people because they recorded details of their lives, government, and religion, and even their popular tall tales, in hieroglyphs, a form of picture writing.

Irrigation

The Egyptians developed methods of stretching their fertile farmlands beyond the riverbanks into the barren desert. They called the rich, dark farmland "black land" and the desert "red land." The painting at top right, from a tomb built 3,300 years ago, shows how a farmer irrigated his fields. With a bucket hung from a pole and balanced with a weight on the other end, he would raise precious water from the low-lying river to an **irrigation** ditch. At right, a modern worker uses the same device—called a "shadoof"— to water his garden.

3000-2700 BC	2700-2200 BC	2000-1660 BC
Early Dynastic Period	**Old Kingdom**	**Middle Kingdom**

Narmer
The tablet below records the origin of the Egyptian state, when the people of Upper and Lower Egypt were conquered by King Narmer. Here the king threatens a defeated enemy. By his side the falcon god Horus, symbol of Upper Egypt, leads a human-headed clump of papyrus, symbolizing Lower Egypt, by the nose!

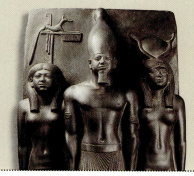

Menkaure
During the Old Kingdom period a succession of famous pharaohs ruled Egypt. Menkaure, shown below with his queen and a goddess, was one of the pyramid builders.

Mentuhotep
After years of internal fighting at the end of the Old Kingdom period, the pharaoh Mentuhotep reunited Egypt. He established a capital at the city of Thebes—modern-day Luxor—and organized a bureaucracy of scribes, tax collectors, and local officials. During his long reign of 51 years he headed military expeditions south to the borders of hostile Nubia.

Egyptians called it simply "the river." Every spring and summer it overflowed its banks, spreading water and rich silt on the fields. Even today, as far as the river's life-giving waters can be stretched by irrigation canals, the land is green and fruitful, turning abruptly into desert where the water ends.

1560-1070 BC
New Kingdom

Hatshepsut, Tutankhamen, and Ramses
At the end of the Middle Kingdom period, foreigners invaded Egypt. After bloody wars to expel them, Egypt's pharaohs resumed power. During the next 500 years some of the famous rulers were Queen Hatshepsut *(left)*, the only female pharaoh; the boy king Tut *(top);* and Ramses II *(right).*

1070-30 BC
Late Period

Cleopatra
The end of Egypt's greatness began with invasions from neighboring countries. Nubians, Assyrians, and Persians ruled in turn, until the armies of Alexander the Great of Greece established a final line of pharaohs, the Ptolemies. Cleopatra VII, the last queen of the Ptolemies, formed an alliance with Julius Caesar, and Egypt became a province of the Roman Empire, never to rise again to its ancient splendor.

Pyramids Ladders to the Sky

Between 2600 and 2200 BC the **pharaohs** built grand pyramids as monumental tombs for themselves. Aligning them along the west bank of the Nile, they raised more than 90 pyramids, ranging from 10 m (33 ft.) to 137 m (450 ft.) high. In the most ancient times, important Egyptians were buried in flat-topped mud-brick buildings called mastabas. Later pharaohs built ever taller structures made of sandstone blocks that would hold their coffins and everything precious they might need in an afterlife. The tallest pyramids were at Giza *(right)*, built for *(from left to right)* Menkaure, Khafre, and Khufu. Inside, dead-end passages and doors made of single stone blocks were meant to confuse thieves and to keep the burial chambers safe. Despite these precautions, the tombs were all found empty.

Inside the Great Pyramid

1. King's Chamber
2. Queen's Chamber
3. Air shaft
4. Grand Gallery and entranceway
5. Dead-end passage

Would You Believe?

A Robot in a Secret Shaft

Although experts have searched every passage in the pyramids, there is still much they don't know. In 1993 a small robot explored a ventilation shaft above the Queen's Chamber in the Great Pyramid. Crawling upward at a 45-degree angle through the 20-cm (8-in.)-wide space, the robot discovered polished limestone in the upper shaft, which ended in a mysterious door. Some believe Pharaoh Khufu's remains could lie hidden behind it. But further searches have been forbidden.

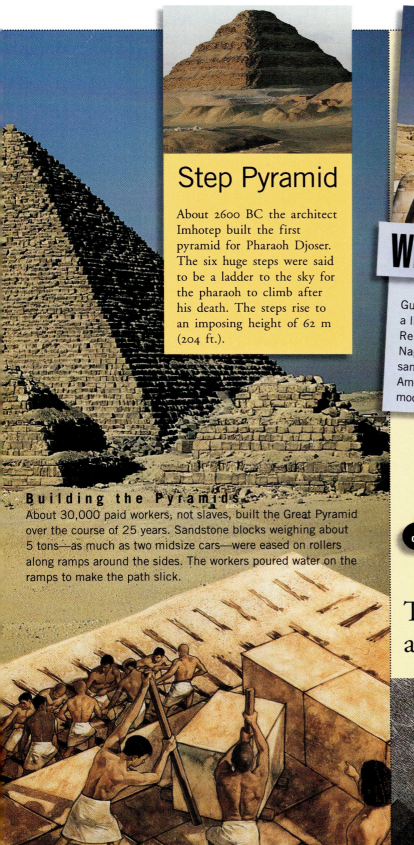

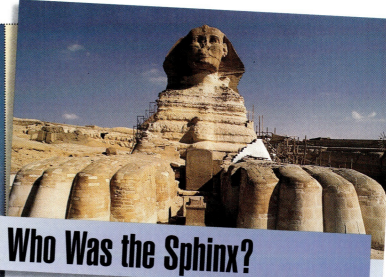

Step Pyramid

About 2600 BC the architect Imhotep built the first pyramid for Pharaoh Djoser. The six huge steps were said to be a ladder to the sky for the pharaoh to climb after his death. The steps rise to an imposing height of 62 m (204 ft.).

Who Was the Sphinx?

Guarding the pyramids at Giza, the 20-m (66-ft.)-high Sphinx has a lion's body and a human's head, but its face is mostly missing. Religious fanatics attacked the nose in the 15th **century**. In 1798 Napoleon's soldiers aimed at the head for target practice. Raging sandstorms scraped the stone and damaged the monument further. American **archaeologist** Mark Lehner used computer-aided design to model the face anew and thinks it may have been Pharaoh Khafre.

Building the Pyramids

About 30,000 paid workers, not slaves, built the Great Pyramid over the course of 25 years. Sandstone blocks weighing about 5 tons—as much as two midsize cars—were eased on rollers along ramps around the sides. The workers poured water on the ramps to make the path slick.

7 Wonders of the World

The Pyramids at Giza

Largest of the **Seven Wonders of the Ancient World,** the pyramids near Cairo, Egypt, are the best preserved today. The Great Pyramid (below, front), built for Pharaoh Khufu about 2500 BC, covers 13 acres —about 12 football fields. For about 3,800 years it was the tallest structure in the world, until medieval cathedral spires in Europe topped it.

Gods and Myths

In the time of the **pharaohs** Egyptians spent every day surrounded by symbols of their religion. They saw their gods in the natural world of the river and the desert. Throughout Egypt's long history the importance of one god or another varied as capital cities changed. People thought the sun rose and set because Re, the sun god, was paddling his boat across the sky. At noontime, they believed, the arch of the sky above them was held up by the sky goddess Nut. And they expected the jackal-headed desert god Anubis to care for them after death. Most families worshiped gods important to their hometown. They also believed in gods who were personal **patrons** of trade, justice, and prosperity.

Sacred Animals

Did the Egyptians really worship cats? Yes, they revered the cat goddess, Bastet, for her help in keeping rats out of the grain bins. The idea of gods with animal heads or bodies began in the most ancient times. Then small tribes adopted familiar animals as their protectors. People living near the river might choose the ibis, a wading bird *(left)*; those on the desert's fringe may have identified with the baboon, a monkey *(above)*. Other animal gods included the female hippopotamus, patron of women in childbirth, and the lion-headed Sekhmet, the powerful mother goddess. Some animals were revered for particular qualities, such as the bull for its strength.

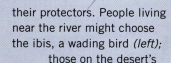

The Gods of Ancient Egypt

The Story of Isis and Osiris

The ancient Egyptian belief revolves around Osiris, god-king of Egypt. He was killed by his wicked brother, Seth, who then became king. Isis, Osiris's wife, found the body, but Seth seized it again, cut it into 14 pieces, and threw them into the Nile. Isis rescued all the pieces, took the form of a bird, and fanned new life into the pieces with her wings. The reborn Osiris then became king of the souls of the dead.

Anubis

Portrayed with the jackal head of a desert scavenger, Anubis, god of embalming, cared for the bodies of the dead.

Daily Journey of the Sun God

Egyptians believed that by day the sun god, Re, shown above as a ram-headed figure, crossed the heavens in his magic boat, and by night he traveled belowground through the underworld. This tomb painting shows Re's nightly journey through a dark landscape and a desert of burning sand, past a cave rumbling with thunder, and across a lake of fire. Humans or gods propel the boat with oars. Many other gods and the spirits of Egyptians who have died ride with the boat. At the start of the new day, when Re reappears above the horizon, the souls of the dead are reborn into new lives with him.

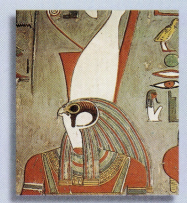

HORUS

Represented with a falcon's head, Horus was the powerful son of Isis and Osiris. The pharaoh was his living counterpart on earth.

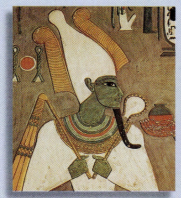

OSIRIS

God of renewal and eternal life, Osiris reigned as supreme judge of the dead. He decided whether a person was worthy of eternal life.

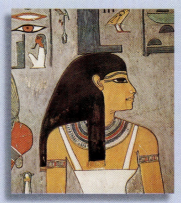

ISIS

Wife of Osiris, Isis protected the dead in her role as perfect wife and mother. She is often represented by wings on the outside of coffins.

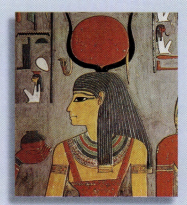

HATHOR

Often shown with a cow's head or wearing a cow-horn headdress, Hathor was the goddess of prosperity, fertility, youth, and beauty.

Strange! But TRUE!

Amulets

Small charms, or amulets, were important to both ordinary Egyptians and the mightiest of the pharaohs. They believed that the charms had power to protect a person.

The **scarab** beetle *(left)* was thought to carry the sun to the heavens. People wanted its protection to take them to heaven as well. The ankh *(top)* symbolized the breath of life. People wore amulets like jewelry. Priests tucked as many as 100 between the mummy wrappings, or placed them with other treasures in the tombs. Tomb robbers sought out the valuable scarabs bound over the hearts of mummies.

Would You Believe?

Light as a Feather

Egyptians thought that after death the soul had to pass a series of tests on its journey to the afterlife. In this tomb painting, a **scribe** faces judgment as his heart is weighed on the balance scale against the Feather of Truth. Anubis handles the scales. If the deceased has lived a truthful, good life, his heart will be light enough for Osiris to reward him with eternal life.

Mysterious Mummies

Egyptian mummies have fascinated the world for hundreds of years. People flock to see them in modern museums, and many movies have featured a scary scene where the mummy wakes. In the most ancient times the dead were simply buried in the hot desert sand, which dried and preserved the bodies well, giving them a mummy-like appearance. Later, belief in an afterlife in which the soul needed a well-preserved body encouraged wealthy Egyptians to look for more splendid ways of keeping dead bodies intact.

By the time of the New Kingdom—3,500 years ago—complicated rituals and procedures had evolved to keep the corpse looking as it had in life. Padding, paint, wigs, special tarlike coatings, and many yards of fine linen wrappings helped achieve this effect.

Beneath the Bandages

The mummy of a wealthy or royal person would not be laid to rest wrapped only in linen strips. Priests tucked protective amulets and personal jewelry between the wrappings. They placed an ornamental mask depicting the person's face over the bandages and laid the body in a coffin. At least one and sometimes more wooden or metal coffins surrounded the first one, each decorated with texts and scenes showing the life of the deceased. Inscriptions might include the texts of spells to help the soul find its way through the underworld. The coffins were then encased in a carved stone **sarcophagus.**

Animal Mummies

The two falcons at left were probably buried in honor of the falcon god, Horus. Egyptians honored their gods by **sacrificing** and mummifying the animals associated with them. Pilgrims journeyed to worship centers to offer wrapped and mummified animals: ibises for Thoth, the god of **scribes;** dogs for Anubis, the god of embalming; and cats for Bastet, the cat goddess.

Ramses II

The mummy of Ramses II has had a lively journey. Embalmed in 1224 BC and first unwrapped in 1886—3,110 years later—it was flown to Paris and opened again for study and repair in 1976. Scientists found the pharaoh had had red hair and suffered from arthritis.

Preserving the Dead

Priestly embalmers prepared the bodies for the afterlife. Wearing the mask of Anubis, as shown at left, they removed stomach, intestines, liver, and lungs and placed them in four special jars carved with the heads of the sons of Horus *(below)*. They removed the brain with a hook through the nose and threw it away. Egyptians believed the heart—not the brain—was the source of personality. Embalmers packed a natural salt called natron into the body cavity to dry it out and stuffed it with straw or cloth. Finally they spread oils and spices on the body and wrapped it in linen strips.

I Was There!

More than 3,000 years after this mummy's death, French scientists studied this and other corpses with modern medical techniques. Their notes showed that *"most of the mummies did not live longer than 30 or 40 years. Their lungs were often filled with sand from desert storms. The bandages showed traces of plant pollen from wheat, barley, nettle, sage, and evergreen shrubs and trees,"* which grew in Egypt so long ago.

Valley of the Kings

Pharaoh Thutmose I knew that most royal tombs—even those inside pyramids—had been robbed and their treasures scattered. To ensure the survival of his own remains, he established a community of masons and artists in a desolate desert valley outside Thebes and had them cut a secret tomb for him right into the rock of the mountainside. Others followed his example, and for more than 400 years mummies were sealed in tombs tunneled into the rocks. Most of the tombs belong to royalty, but there are also a few for wealthy officials. Workers from the village of Deir el-Medina used only stone and copper tools in the shafts, hauling broken pieces out in baskets. They covered the walls of the burial chamber with plaster and decorated them with texts and pictures. Painting only with black, white, yellow, green, blue, and red pigments, they produced the amazing pictures we can still see today. In the utter blackness of inner rooms, all work was done by the light of oil lamps.

Architecture of Eternity

The pyramids may have been built to mirror mountains, but this peak towers like a natural pyramid over the tombs in the Valley of the Kings. Camouflaged entrances to the shafts in the rock were soon covered with shifting sand and rubble from the construction of later tombs. As a result, early modern explorers found entrances only by accident, after noticing depressions in the ground or mysterious clefts in the rough rock walls. Nowadays archaeologists use radar scanning gear to probe the limits of unexplored tomb chambers.

Provisions for the Afterlife

Gold Box

When **archaeologist** Howard Carter poked his candle through a hole in a tomb doorway in 1922 he saw "strange animals, statues, and gold. Everywhere the glint of gold." He was describing the richest **cache** of Egyptian **artifacts** ever found: the tomb of Tutankhamen. King Tut's tomb had been opened before by robbers, who were probably interrupted during the raid, for most of his funerary hoard was in disarray but still intact. As fresh air entered the chambers during Carter's searches, ancient objects fashioned from leather, fabrics, and other **organic** materials crumbled into dust. They and the thousands of objects that

Anubis

Would You Believe?

The Mummy's Curse

When excavation patron Lord Carnarvon died soon after visiting Tut's tomb, newspaper headlines screamed that the mummy had cursed him for disturbing the pharaoh's peace. The press claimed 24 more victims for the curse—but archaeologist Carter was unharmed, and the doctor who examined the mummy lived into his 80s.

A Rich Burial

Tutankhamen's quartzite **sarcophagus** contained three inner coffins, two of gilded wood and the last one of solid gold. The mummy wore a pure gold mask detailed with glass, quartz, and obsidian. On one wall 12 baboons represent the 12 hours of the night that Tut must pass on Re's boat before rebirth at dawn. On the other wall, Tut meets Osiris and the sky goddess Nut.

Throne

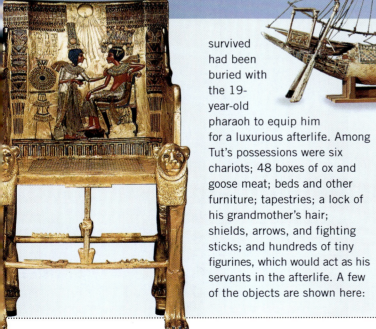

Model Boat

survived had been buried with the 19-year-old pharaoh to equip him for a luxurious afterlife. Among Tut's possessions were six chariots; 48 boxes of ox and goose meat; beds and other furniture; tapestries; a lock of his grandmother's hair; shields, arrows, and fighting sticks; and hundreds of tiny figurines, which would act as his servants in the afterlife. A few of the objects are shown here:

The elegant Anubis statue at far left stood guard over the tomb to ensure the favor and protection of the jackal-headed god. The bejeweled golden box held perfumed ointment; but when it was opened, the ointment had turned into a foul-smelling brown goo. Tut's royal throne was made of wood covered in a thin layer of gold. The scene on the back depicts Tut's queen, Ankhesenamen, anointing him with oil. The golden boat was

to carry him safely through the underworld. And the painted chest shows a war-like Tutankhamen attacking Nubians from his chariot, but he probably never fought a battle.

Chest

The Lost Tomb

I n the 1850s an English **Egyptologist** discovered a tomb in the Valley of the Kings, which he noted as "KV5" for Kings' Valley No. 5. He remarked that it had been robbed and moved to other sites. Shifting sands and **excavation** work in the valley buried KV5's entrance, and it lay forgotten until American **archaeologist** Kent R. Weeks uncovered it in 1989 near King Tut's tomb. Hasty exploration had shown the corridor leading into KV5 was a mess of rubble left by leaking walls and long-ago tomb robbers. But Weeks looked at the place again in 1995 just as it was about to be bulldozed for a bus turn-around. He found an unopened door leading to more corridors and many debris-filled chambers—in fact, it is the largest tomb discovered yet, and may have up to 150 rooms. And treasure? Well, so far the thousands of **shards,** glazed beads, broken jars, and furniture pieces are not the richest loot ever discovered, but they are invaluable to archaeologists. Going by inscriptions, Weeks believes KV5 was built for the burial of some of Ramses II's 50 sons.

Fast FACTS

Tips on Tombs in Kings' Valley

How Many? Sixty-two tombs have been found. But archaeologists believe there may be as many as 4,000 undiscovered ones.

How Old? The tombs in the Valley of the Kings were built during the New Kingdom more than 3,000 years ago.

Largest KV5 is the largest tomb explored so far, with as many as 150 chambers, built on several levels.

Richest King Tutankhamen's tomb, KV62, contained the most objects, including precious gold and jeweled items.

Who Was Buried There? Pharaohs, some queens, and high officials.

Digging Up the Past

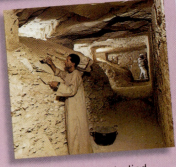

C leaning out the rubble that is piled to the ceiling is a huge job. Forty-two workmen start at 6:00 a.m., breaking up pieces and carrying them out in baskets—up to 9 tons per day! All this material is sifted to make sure nothing valuable is missed. Artists draw all the plaster and pottery fragments to help reconstruct the decorations of the tomb. Photographers, architects, surveyors, geologists, and engineers have been called in, too. They have studied and mapped the layout and propped up the dangerously cracked walls and ceilings so that the tomb is safe to work in.

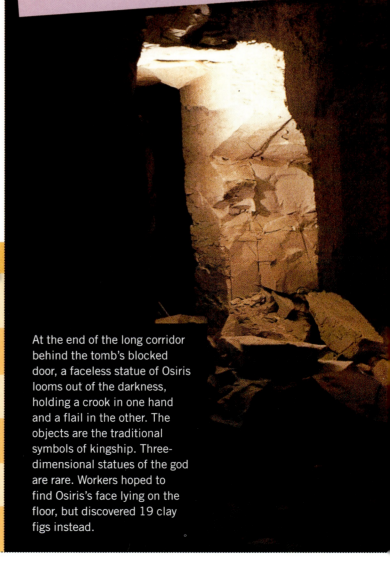

At the end of the long corridor behind the tomb's blocked door, a faceless statue of Osiris looms out of the darkness, holding a crook in one hand and a flail in the other. The objects are the traditional symbols of kingship. Three-dimensional statues of the god are rare. Workers hoped to find Osiris's face lying on the floor, but discovered 19 clay figs instead.

108 Rooms and No End in Sight!

As workers dig through the tomb and do engineering studies, they are finding more and more rooms *(diagram at right)*. So far they have discovered 108 chambers. A sloping stairway leads to a blank wall, but vibrating floors on the main level encourage the idea that there may be more levels under- neath. The pillared hall at the entrance of the tomb is enormous, measuring 15 by 15 m (50 by 50 ft.). Fifteen of the pillars were cut out of solid rock, but the 16th is a plastered stone fake. The rooms are filled with rubble to the ceiling, and it will take decades more before the entire tomb is cleared.

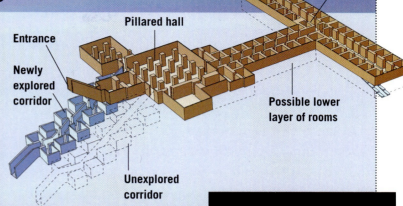

Statue of Osiris

Pillared hall

Entrance

Newly explored corridor

Possible lower layer of rooms

Unexplored corridor

People

Kent Weeks

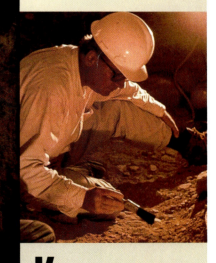

Kent Weeks happily endures dust, 48°C (120°F) heat, and the problems of conserving and identifying **artifacts** as he delves into KV5. In fact, the American University of Cairo archaeologist is looking forward to spending the rest of his life on the project. Six days a week in summer (resting on Friday, the Muslim Sabbath) his team works at the site from 6:00 a.m. to 1:00 p.m., then spends afternoons writing, drawing, and preparing materials to help reconstruct the past.

Temples for the God-Kings

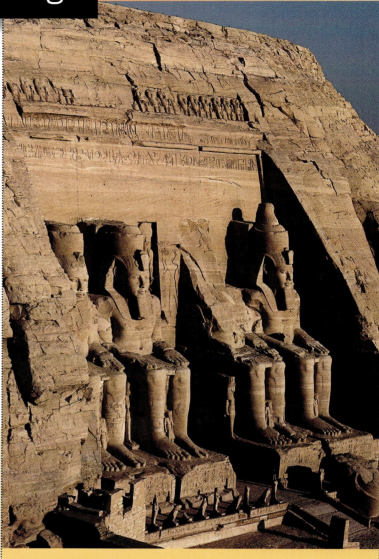

The ordinary people in ancient Egypt dedicated offerings to the gods and wrote spells and requests to ensure a god's favor. But they didn't attend weekly services in the magnificent temples. Those temples were reserved for the images of the gods—including portraits of **pharaohs** who became gods after death—and their priestly servants. Each temple was centered on the worship of a single god but might also include shrines for others: Amun-Re shared a shrine with his wife, Mut, in the immense complex of Karnak, across the river from the Valley of the Kings. Other temples served the goddess Hathor. One pharaoh ordered the building of a temple, and later pharaohs added more courts, columned halls, and gateways, so the structures grew over the years. Supplying such a place with workmen, food, linens, and all the necessities of life was the daily business of the surrounding villages.

Priestly Duties

Inside a temple, a priest of Amun-Re waves a bowl of incense *(top left)*. The priest's daily rituals secured the god's favor and ensured the well-being of the Egyptian state. Three times a day priests approached the statue of the god, bathed it, dressed it, and served it food and drink. When the statue had eaten its fill, the priests got to eat the "leftovers." The temple staff managed the surrounding fields, oversaw construction projects, and made repairs to the buildings. The temples also served as storage places. In the painting at bottom left, a **scribe** records incoming supplies weighed by temple servants.

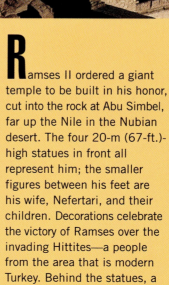

Ramses II ordered a giant temple to be built in his honor, cut into the rock at Abu Simbel, far up the Nile in the Nubian desert. The four 20-m (67-ft.)-high statues in front all represent him; the smaller figures between his feet are his wife, Nefertari, and their children. Decorations celebrate the victory of Ramses over the invading Hittites—a people from the area that is modern Turkey. Behind the statues, a corridor leads to a sanctuary for another statue of Ramses. Twice a year, shafts of sunlight stream into the interior and light up his face. Between 1964 and 1968, when the Aswan High Dam was built on the Nile, the dammed-up waters created Lake Nasser, which endangered this monument. Engineers cut away the entire temple from the hill, sawed it into pieces, and reassembled it on higher ground.

Karnak

Now serene ruins *(left)*, the once busy complex of Amun-Re's temple at Karnak *(inset)* centered on a sacred lake, surrounded by chapels and **obelisks** to honor the gods. The temple community dominated a mile-long stretch of the Nile that connected it to a second shrine at Luxor. In ancient times people celebrated religious holidays near the temples. They joined parades led by the priests to the cemetery, where they left offerings for their dead.

Hatshepsut

Funerary Temples

Though they were buried in the Valley of the Kings, pharaohs built temples elsewhere to honor their remains. Queen Hatshepsut's shrine at Deir el-Bahri *(right)* is nestled into the mountain behind the Valley of the Kings. The temple walls are lined with images telling of her achievements. Her successor, Thutmose III, had her face scraped off from most of the paintings, hoping to erase her fame as well.

Confident and capable, Queen Hatshepsut declared herself pharaoh and ruled Egypt in place of her stepson, young Thutmose III. Most of her portrait monuments show her as a man, as above, wearing men's clothing and a false beard.

Everyday Life

Egyptian tombs are decorated with scenes of daily life because the ancient Egyptians hoped to live the same life after death in the afterlife. Paintings show parents and children together at meals, performing religious duties, or enjoying a day's hunting in the Nile marshes. Boys and some girls from wealthy families learned reading and writing from **scribes.** People ate three meals a day: cereals, stewed fruit, fish, beef, wheat bread, and sweets made with dates and honey. They were concerned about their appearance and washed often; men shaved, and everyone did their hair carefully. Eyeliner protected eyelids from pesky Egyptian flies. Women dressed in simple linen shifts, and men wore short skirtlike garments. Young children wore nothing.

A Life of Leisure

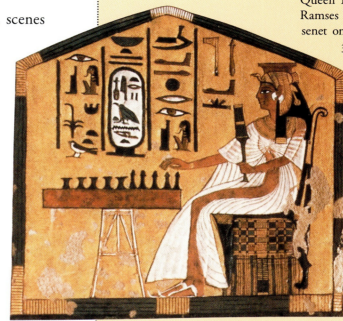

Queen Nefertari, wife of Ramses II, plays a game of senet on a board marked into 30 squares, in this scene from her tomb. To get the next move for her carved pieces, she would have thrown short sticks as we might throw dice. Many of the game sets were made of ivory, ebony, or precious metal. Besides playing board games, royal entertainment included music, dance, and storytelling.

Children's Games

No one who is alive today remembers the rules for piggyback catch, played by the girls below. Teammates may have switched position when a player dropped the ball. Boys and girls usually played separately. The boys of wealthy families learned archery and horsemanship. Others held high-jump and tug of war contests or threw arrowlike sticks at targets.

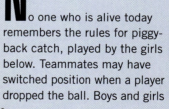

Imagine That!

Family Pets

A cat herding geese, similar to a bird dog bringing in birds for its hunting master, on the painting at left, shows how much Egyptians treasured their pets. Cats were held dear for their usefulness in keeping grain free of rats and mice. When pet cats died, members of a family shaved their eyebrows in mourning. Dogs rated high as pets, too. A tombstone inscribed with a picture of a dog and the name "Neb" adorns the grave of a pet in an Old Kingdom burial ground. Egyptians bred greyhounds, salukis, and sheepdogs. Nobles often kept monkeys and gazelles.

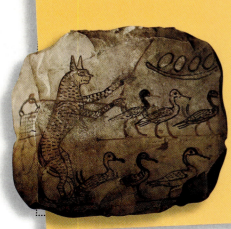

At Home

In the **papyrus** painting above, a wealthy couple stands before its country home. The house has high windows for privacy and for keeping out dust; roof vents and white-washed walls help against the Egyptian heat. The homes of the well-to-do always included a garden with date palms, pomegranate bushes, and a fishpond. The interior scene at right is a hive of activity: Servants prepare and carry food while the master receives guests on the first floor.

Children's Toys

Playthings have not changed a lot. Besides inventing whirling games and enjoying board games, Egyptian children played with toys like these.

Balls
These brightly colored fabric balls were made for young children. The insides are stuffed with material just like that of a modern softball. Ancient balls were also made of wood or clay.

Pull Toy
This wooden cat could open and close its mouth when a child pulled on the string.

Paddle Doll
The doll at right wears a fine pleated dress, with a checked hem and jeweled collar, all painted on. Her luxuriant fiber curls have lasted thousands of years without a single trip to the hairdresser.

What Are Hieroglyphs?

Hieroglyph is a Greek word meaning "sacred carving"—a good description of this Egyptian writing system. Hieroglyphic texts carved on the walls of tombs were meant to protect the dead. The symbols listed the good deeds of their life on earth and provided strong spells for guidance through the dangerous underworld. Few Egyptians could write, because there were more than 700 signs to be learned. Those who were literate held real power: **Scribes** were respected employees of the state. When Egyptians adopted Christianity in the Roman era in the third **century** AD, they abandoned hieroglyphs. No one could read the signs until 1822, when Frenchman Jean-François Champollion studied inscriptions on stone written in Egyptian hieroglyphs and Greek and was able to translate them.

"Be a Scribe!"

Sitting cross legged and holding a sheet of **papyrus** on his lap, the statue of a scribe looks ready for dictation. Ancient scribe Khety encouraged his son to become a scribe, too, because *"metalworkers smell worse than rotten fish, contractors get dirty from carrying mud. There's no job without an overseer except the scribe's: he is the overseer."*

Papyrus: the First Paper

Papyrus, a thick reed that grows on the banks of the Nile, was made into the first kind of writing paper. Workers peeled off the outer stem of the reed and slit the inner fibers into thin strips. They laid the strips together on a hard surface and beat them with a mallet until the fibers fused into a solid, damp mat. This was weighted down for several days and dried into a single sheet. A scribe smoothed out any roughness with a polishing stone before he wrote on the papyrus. Inscribed papyrus was often rolled into scrolls.

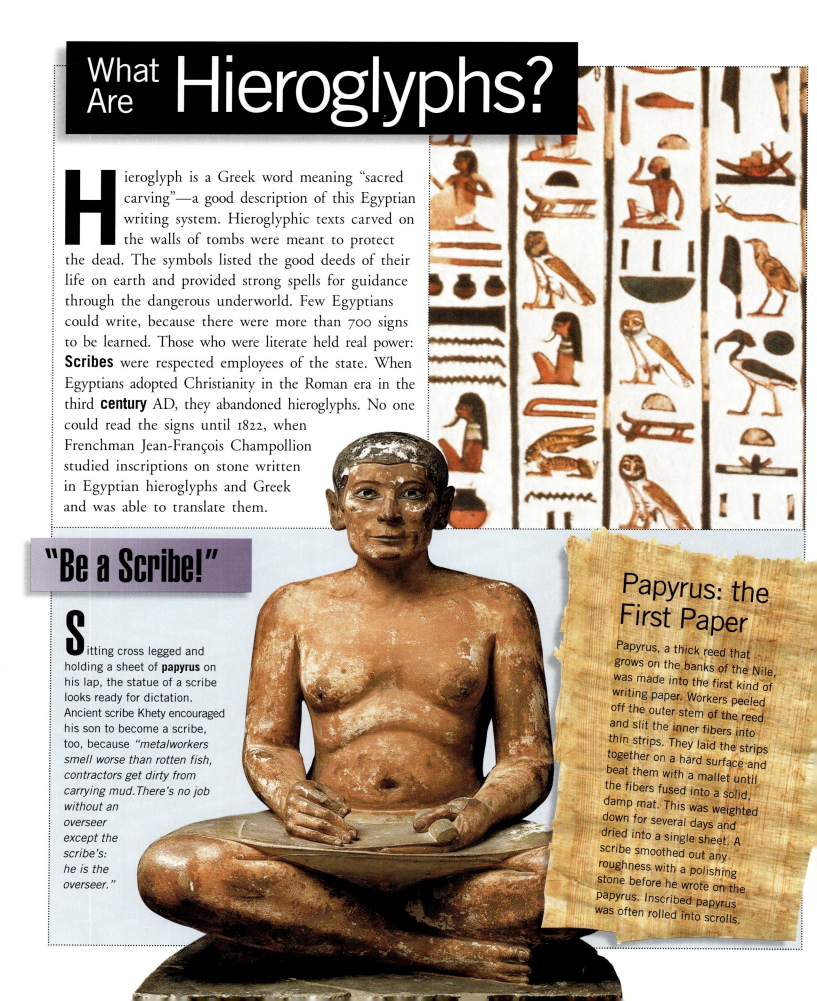

Try it!

Write Your Name in Hieroglyphs

Hieroglyphs evolved from small pictures of things, most of which we can still recognize. Some pictures stood for sounds, like letters in our alphabet. Others indicated something about the sense of the word—for instance, if it had feet attached, it was a word involving motion. The hieroglyphs don't correspond exactly to the alphabet for English, though; in Egyptian "f" and "v" sound the same, as do "r" and "l," so there was only a single sign for each of these. (But the letter "l," shown as a lion here, was added later.) There is no sign for our letter "e," because Egyptian only needed an "i" sound; nor is there a letter "o," because vowels aren't always spelled out. Sometimes the figure characters like the vulture face one way, sometimes another. This tells you which way the inscription is written. Using the chart at right you can write your own name. If you have a choice of signs, use the nicest-looking one.

The Royal Names

Royal names were written inside a magic loop of rope called a **cartouche.** Here you see the cross on top of a circle, which represents "nfr." The standing reed is "i." The loaf at top is "t," the mouth below it "r," and the double reeds below that "y"—making up the name of Queen Nefertari.

a	vulture		l	lion	
b	foot		m	owl	
ch sh	lake		n	water Nile	
d	hand		nfr	triconsonant	
f	horned viper		p	mat	
g	pot		q	hill	
h	shelter		r	open mouth	
h	twisted rope		s/z	door bolt	
i	reed leaf		s/c	folded cloth	
j/dj	cobra		t	bread loaf	
k	basket		tj ch	tethering rope	
kh	sieve		ou w	chick	
kh	cow's belly		y	two reeds	

P a t r i c i a = P a t r i c h a

A l e x a n d e r = A l x a n d r

Other Scripts

Simpler forms of writing, developed from hieroglyphs that were written quickly—like our cursive—were called hieratic and demotic. Hieroglyphs were drawn carefully and look the same no matter who carved them, but hieratic and demotic reflect the different handwritings of the scribes who penned them. They were used for recording events, taxes, poems, and other texts. So many of these scrolls have survived that hundreds are still untranslated.

Nubia Egypt's Rival

Hemmed in by deserts to the east and west and the Mediterranean Sea in the north, ancient Egypt was well protected from enemy invasions. But the country was always open to attack from Nubia, the country to the south, on land that today belongs partly to Egypt, partly to Sudan. Where the broad valley narrows south of the first **cataract,** the landscape changes. The climate is drier and hotter there, and crops do not grow as bountifully as in Egypt. From earliest times Egypt traded with Nubia, sending grain, honey, cotton fabric, copper tools, and oil in exchange for spices, copper ore, gold, and timber. As early as 3000 BC the Egyptians began to raid the upper Nile and seize precious copper and gold.

Eventually Egypt invaded Nubian territory and secured it with military forts. The Egyptians respected the fighting abilities of Nubians and often hired them as **mercenary** soldiers. Different tribal groups moved in and out of the country over the next few hundred years, so the kingdoms of Nubia, and their relations with Egypt, were constantly changing. During periods of internal Egyptian turmoil Nubians retaliated and invaded Egypt. The Nubian kingdom at Meroë outlasted pharaonic Egypt by about 500 years.

What's an Archaeologist?

Archaeologists dig up buried **artifacts** of people who lived a long time ago. Besides carefully removing and preserving artifacts, **archaeologists** have to interpret what they find. Bit by bit they can piece together a people's history. To do this right, they have to wear many different hats. They have to be:

Linguists
Historians
Art Experts
Detectives
Spelunkers
Biologists
Architects
Divers
and
Engineers

Nubian Warriors

Forming an impressive squadron of bodyguards, these figures of Nubian bowmen were found among the grave goods of an Egyptian buried about 2000 BC. Often used as scouts or interpreters, the Nubians were also famous archers, and their country was known as the Land of the Bow. In peaceful times Nubians were hired by Egypt to guard the tombs in the Valley of the Kings and to prevent robbers from plundering the royal tombs—but many clever thieves succeeded anyway.

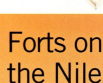

Forts on the Nile

Middle Kingdom **pharaohs** built the forts at Semna and Kumma along the upper river now in ruins *(left)* to stop Nubian expansion. Troops stationed there with their families kept watch on the river and nearby lands. The drawing at top reconstructs how they may have looked.

Bearing Gifts of Gold

Southern riches sold by the Nubians were so attractive to the Old Kingdom Egyptians that they built canals near the first cataract to make shipping easier. The Nubian traders sold gold from their mines and acted as middlemen for exotic African products like leopard and giraffe skins, ostrich feathers, and ivory. Caravans of pack donkeys brought the precious cargoes to the river from the African interior. In the painting at left, Nubians dressed in linen and leopard skins offer a selection of treasures.

Nubia Close up

After a trip on the Nile in the fifth **century** BC, the Greek Herodotus marveled at the Nubians. Calling them the tallest and handsomest people he had ever seen, he said they ate only meat and milk, and lived to the age of 120. In spite of such praises, the region was forgotten by scholars for centuries and changed names many times. Between 2000 BC and AD 500 the Nubian kingdoms were known as Yam, Kush, Napata, Meroë, and Ethiopia. At the time when Egyptian forts on the Nile controlled the borderlands, young Nubian princes were sent to be educated at the court of the **pharaoh** and adopted Egyptian customs. After the fall of the New Kingdom, Nubian warlords Piye and Shabaka marched down the river in the eighth century BC and conquered Egypt. Under Nubian rule the combined kingdoms became the largest of ancient Africa, until Assyrians, Persians, and Greeks in turn overran Lower Egypt. Independent Nubian **civilizations** continued to flourish, smelting iron and developing an alphabet, but Nubia's ancient language has been forgotten.

Warriors

Portrayed on a temple wall relief, this Nubian wears a chain-mail shirt and heavy collar to deflect enemy arrows and spears. The fearsome reputation of Nubian soldiers inspired Middle Kingdom priests to turn to magic for help against them, writing the words "Kush" and "Ruler of Kush" on clay tablets, which they then smashed. Later pharaohs drew pictures of Nubians on their sandal soles, so they would be ground underfoot.

King Taharqa

The powerful king of Egypt and Nubia, Taharqa, was buried with pomp and possessions. This .61-m (2-ft.)-high shawabti (a figure said to carry out one's tasks in the afterlife) carved in Taharqa's image shows his African features with the formal beard of a pharaoh.

Pyramid Power!

There are more pyramids in modern-day Sudan, once the land of Nubia, than in Egypt! Each of these steep-sided brick pyramids near the fourth **cataract** covers the tomb of a wealthy or royal person. Built 1,500 years after the Great Pyramid of Khufu, they are much smaller; most are less than 15 m (50 ft.) high. Few have been explored to date.

Treasures of a Queen

This precious shield ring was fashioned from gold that wasn't traded but stayed in Nubia. The design features the head of the god Amun-Re bedecked with a triple necklace, symbolizing kingship. Queen Amanishakheto of Meroë wore it—as a decoration on her forehead, not her finger—before it went with her into her tomb. The ring is part of the rich hoard of gold that is the only treasure ever found in the pyramids of Meroë.

Meroë

The Ptolemies, Greek rulers of Egypt from 332 to 30 BC, renewed the lively trade with Nubia. The kingdom they recognized centered on a place called Meroë, far up on the east bank of the Nile where land was fertile enough to graze herds and grow many crops. Furnaces there processed iron for tools and weapons that were much stronger than the bronze and wood used in Egypt. Meroë was close to the old caravan trail from the south, and traders specialized in gold, ivory, and live elephants. Royal power was sometimes shared by a queen. Meroë's craftsmen made a great variety of beautiful objects, featuring African animals and symbols, like the giraffes and snakes on the pot above.

Indus Valley Civilization

More than 6,000 years ago, present-day Pakistan and western India were inhabited by **nomadic** herders. Each winter they brought their herds down from the mountains to feed in the Indus River Valley. Gradually the herders turned to farming and began to live in the valley year round. By 2500 BC they had built many villages and towns, as well as two cities, Harappa and Mohenjo-Daro.

These communities had long, straight streets lined with mud-brick houses and shops, including public baths *(right)*. To protect against floods, the inhabitants built many buildings on mounds of earth and rubble. For almost 600 years they flourished, at one time controlling more than twice as much territory as the people of Mesopotamia. Then, about 1900 BC, the Indus people departed, perhaps because of a drought. They never returned.

A House in Harappa

At one time 35,000 people lived in Harappa. Houses were often two stories high and had many rooms. Each house was built around a central courtyard where meals were cooked and eaten. Each house also had an indoor bathroom, and wastewater flowed into street sewers, an invention not known until then.

Then & NOW!

A Common Ritual

A 5,000-year-old Indus statue of a woman *(left)* shows the faint stains of dyes used in ancient worship ceremonies. Hindu women still mark their foreheads with a red dye during daily prayers *(above)*.

INDUS VALLEY
Mohenjo-Daro • Indus R. • Harappa

The Great Bath

The spectacular Great Bath of Mohenjo-Daro was built on a high mound of dirt and brick. Its central pool was surrounded by several meeting halls. The Indus people probably used the bath for religious rituals.

Who Was He?

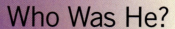

The statue below may be of a beloved or a feared king. **Archaeologists** have found no evidence that the Indus people were ruled by kings or anyone who was in power very long. Some scholars think that the government was instead run by groups of wealthy merchants, landowners, or religious leaders.

Mysterious Script

The Indus people had a unique form of writing that used pictures (especially of animals) and strange symbols. This script has been found on more than 4,000 objects, including many seals once used by potters to stamp their goods *(right)*. Unfortunately, scholars have not been able to decipher the writing, so no one knows what the symbols mean. If the code is ever broken, many questions—Did they have kings? What gods or goddesses did they worship? Why didn't they build palaces or temples?—may finally be answered.

Ancient Playthings

Indus craftsmen used clay to make many everyday objects, including playthings for children and adults. A child probably played with the toy cart below. It has a driver and oxen like the real ones that once carried goods and people along the wide streets of the great Indus cities. Adults probably used the dice at right for gambling. The 4,000-year-old dice are marked like those of today, but the numbers are in a different order.

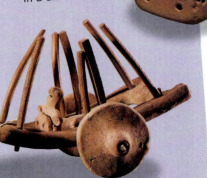

What Is Hinduism?

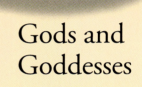

Shiva

Hinduism may be the world's oldest religion still in existence. Its beginnings can be traced back at least 4,000 years, when Sanskrit-speaking nomads from central Asia invaded India. They settled in the Ganges Valley, where **monsoon** rains gave rise to fertile farmland. Some people from the Indus Valley may have migrated there when their rivers began to dry up. The nomads brought their religion. They also adopted some of the religious beliefs and practices of the people living there. From this mixture Hinduism developed.

Hinduism has no fixed teachings or single way of worshiping. Most Hindus believe that everything is part of one truth, called Brahman. But they worship many different likenesses of gods. Hindus also believe in **reincarnation**—the belief that when you die you are reborn into another body.

Gods and Goddesses

Two of Hinduism's most popular gods are Shiva and Vishnu. Vishnu *(left)* is the protector of the world. He is said to have come down to earth 10 times in different forms. Once he came as the god Krishna, and the next time as the Buddha—founder of the religion Buddhism *(pages 50-51)*.

Shiva *(above)* is the god who destroys ignorance. He is often shown with four arms, encircled by flames. His many arms are a symbol of his power.

Hindus also pray to a mother goddess who takes many forms and has many names. Shiva's wife, Durga, destroys evil and showers earth with flowers. Vishnu's wife, Lakshmi, blesses people with success, wealth, and virtue.

Vishnu

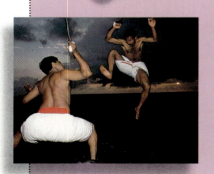

Holy River

Hindus believe that India's Ganges River is holy. They call it Ganga Ma, or "Mother Ganges." According to Hindu legend, the river was sent to earth from heaven to clean people's souls. Millions of Hindus take religious baths in its sacred waters each year.

The Caste System

The ancient Hindus divided people into four main social groups, or **castes.** In the highest were scholars and priests. Next came rulers and warriors, then merchants and farmers, and finally, peasants and servants.

Beneath all these castes were the "untouchables." It was believed that people of higher castes would become unclean if they touched them.

For centuries, people were locked in the caste into which they were born. In modern India, however, this rigid social system has weakened. People mix more freely with each other. Treating someone as an "untouchable" is now against the law.

Priest

Warrior

Farmer

Laborer

Then & NOW!

Hindu Rituals

For thousands of years, Hindus have marked important events with religious rituals. Families have special naming celebrations for their babies when they are about 10 days old. Religious ceremonies are also performed when a boy gets his first haircut and when a girl's ears are pierced.

Hindu weddings last for hours. An important part of the ceremony is when the wedding couple sits in front of a fire *(left)*. The groom says to his bride, "Be my friend. Let's love each other and protect each other. Let's live together for a hundred autumns."

Hindus do not bury their dead. Bodies are cremated, or burned. If possible, the ashes are scattered in a river.

What Is Buddhism?

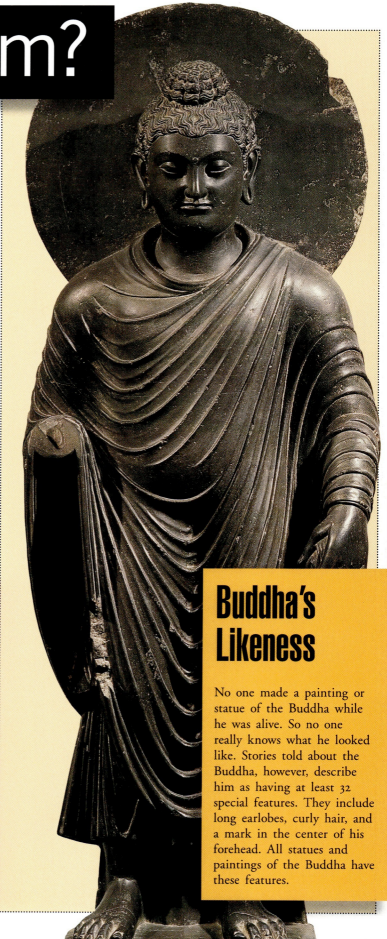

Siddhartha Gautama, born in the sixth **century** BC near the northern border of India, was a wealthy Hindu prince with a beautiful wife and child but became deeply troubled by the suffering he saw outside his palace. He decided to give up everything he owned and seek an answer to why life was so hard. Siddhartha wandered through

CHINA
•Bamiyan
Sanchi
•Ajanta
INDIA

Spread of Buddhism

India for many years. One day, while meditating, he experienced enlightenment. He realized that there is always suffering in the world, that the suffering comes from wanting things, and that when a person stops wanting, the suffering stops. He prescribed eight "right" ways of thinking to help people enter a state of bliss he called **nirvana.** One way involved daily **meditation.** Siddhartha soon had many followers, who called him Buddha, which means "enlightened one." After his death in about 483 BC, his teachings—Buddhism—spread from India farther east in Asia.

Taming the Wild Elephant

This stone carving tells a famous story about the Buddha. An Indian ruler disliked the Buddha's teachings and wanted him killed. He arranged to have ferocious elephants charge at him. But as the elephants rushed forward, he spoke lovingly to them and they dropped peacefully to their knees.

Buddha's Likeness

No one made a painting or statue of the Buddha while he was alive. So no one really knows what he looked like. Stories told about the Buddha, however, describe him as having at least 32 special features. They include long earlobes, curly hair, and a mark in the center of his forehead. All statues and paintings of the Buddha have these features.

More Than a Tomb

One of the most famous early followers of the Buddha was the third-century BC Indian emperor Asoka *(page 52).* He built a huge domed structure called a **stupa** (which means "mound") near the village of Sanchi in northern India. This shrine is said to contain some of the Buddha's cremated remains. The stupa represents nirvana—the soul's release from suffering.

Walking on Fire

In an annual ritual, modern Buddhist monks at a monastery in Tibet walk over flaming coals. They come through the ordeal unharmed. In the ancient ceremony participants seek purification and God's blessing. Monks begin studies of the Buddha's sacred teachings by age eight and will become full monks when they are 18 years old.

Buddhist Temples

Sometime in the third century AD, Buddhist monks carved a great monastery from the cliffs in the Bamian River Valley in Afghanistan. They dug out many cavelike rooms and connected them with tunnels. By AD 400, more than 1,000 monks lived in this unusual monastery. Many Buddhists, including kings and princes, made special trips to see it. No one lives in there today, but people still come to see its beautiful paintings and carvings, including a huge statue of the Buddha in the center.

India's Mauryan and Gupta Empires

ndia was divided into several small kingdoms until the third **century** BC, when a young, brash Indian nobleman named Chandragupta Maurya conquered most of the country and declared himself emperor. Thus began India's great Mauryan **dynasty,** which lasted for 137 years.

Much of the dynasty's greatness is attributed to its final emperor, Asoka. During the first 10 years of his reign, Asoka was a cruel, brutal ruler. But after a particularly bloody battle in which 100,000 people died, Asoka had a profound change of heart. He gave up violence and accepted the peaceful teachings of Buddhism. For the final 30 years of his life, Asoka ruled with compassion.

Soon after Asoka's death, the Mauryan **empire** crumbled. India once again became a land of many small kingdoms. About AD 320, a ruler with the same name as the first great Mauryan emperor—Chandragupta —took over much of India. He founded the Gupta dynasty, which lasted for 200 years.

Under Gupta rule, India became one of the most advanced, prosperous, and tolerant countries in the world. Its people enjoyed many freedoms, including freedom of religion. Although Gupta rulers were Hindus, they did not protest against anyone who remained a Buddhist. Their empire would last well into the sixth century.

Brahmi Script

For hundreds of years only priests and scholars could read Sanskrit, the ancient language of India, shown in its Brahmi script above. But that changed during the Gupta dynasty, when upper-**caste** boys were allowed to go to school. As a result, literature and poetry became popular. During poetry tournaments each writer was assigned a theme. The contestant who came up with the cleverest poem based on that theme received a prize. The poets were greatly skilled. One winning poem, for example, said one thing when read left to right and something quite different when read right to left.

National Emblem

Perhaps the most famous sculpture in India is the four-lion capital *(left)* that once crowned a gigantic 50-ton pillar built during Emperor Asoka's reign. Asoka had many of these pillars erected throughout India. They were decorated with Buddhist symbols and sayings. The pillars were also carved with the inspirational teachings of Asoka. He wanted the pillars to remind Indian people to practice truth, compassion, and tolerance.

The four-lion capital is now the national emblem of India. Its picture appears on all Indian coins and bills *(above).*

Epic Poem

The Hindu god Krishna *(blue face)* is shown in battle with the warrior Arjuna in this painting from the Mahabharata. Three times longer than the Bible, it is the world's longest poem.

Would You Believe?

Ahead of Their Time

Gupta mathematicians discovered the concept of zero and developed the decimal system of numbers. Can you read the numbers one through zero below? In fact, the numbers we use come from Hindu and Arabic script.

A Luxurious Lifestyle

The great wealth of the Gupta empire can be seen on paintings drawn by monks 1,500 years ago on the walls of a cave monastery near Ajanta. The Buddhist saint in this painting wears a gold crown and a pearl-and-sapphire necklace. It is the kind of precious jewelry that Gupta princes wore.

Holi Festival

During the annual Holi Festival, young people douse one another with liquid dyes. This ancient celebration marks the beginning of spring. It also commemorates the death of an evil female demon named Holika.

China All-Powerful Emperors

A man so cruel that he was said to have "the heart of a tiger" united various states in China into one **empire** in 221 BC. After crushing his enemies, he named himself Shihuangdi, First Emperor of the Qin. To ensure that no one would rebel against him, he had all weapons collected, melted down, and cast into bells and statues.

The first Chinese people had settled thousands of years earlier along the Yellow River Valley to farm wheat and **millet.** About 2200 BC, the Xia **dynasty** established Chinese traditions. In the Shang dynasty, people built walled towns and palaces, invented writing, and left records. The rulers of the Zhou dynasty extended their kingdom to the Yangzi River Valley, but soon the country split into warring states. Shihuangdi reunified the country and established a system of rule by emperors that would last for more than 2,000 years.

Shang Mask

The lifelike Chinese bronze mask above was made more than 3,000 years ago, when the Shang dynasty ruled northern China. With the Shang came a period of great innovations: They perfected the wheel, spun silk, and cast some of the finest bronze objects ever known. The mask was discovered in an ancient tomb along with the headless skeletons at left. Shang rulers had the men's heads chopped off with axes like the one below to have the victims serve them in the afterlife.

Shang Ax

All-Under-Heaven

Surrounded by deserts, oceans, and mountains, China was isolated from the rest of the world. Not knowing what lay beyond their land, the ancient Chinese thought that they were at the center of the world. They referred to their country as "All-Under-Heaven," or the "Middle Kingdom," the symbol for which is shown at right.

What's a Dynasty?

A dynasty is a ruling family that passes along power from one relative to the next. Chinese history is divided into many different dynasties, with the last one ending in 1912. Some of the earliest dynasties, described in this book, are shown below. The Qin, pronounced "Chin," gave China its name.

1766 BC – 1122 BC	Shang dynasty
1100 BC – 256 BC	Zhou dynasty
221 BC – 206 BC	Qin dynasty
206 BC – AD 220	Han dynasty

The Emperor's Cruel Code

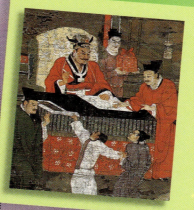

"Boil him alive! Cut off his nose! Tear out a rib!" So spoke the judges at the court of the First Emperor if you committed a crime. The emperor established a harsh set of rules through all of China. Not only would the offender be punished, but so would his entire family!

The Tiger of Qin

Chinese emperors were rich and powerful, and they believed they would be the same in their life after death. Instead of a following of beheaded humans as in Shang times *(opposite)*, the First Emperor had an army made of terra cotta, or clay, to serve him in the afterlife. As many as 10,000 life-size soldiers and horses, some pulling chariots, have stood guard near his tomb since 210 BC.

Oracle Bones and Books

Before you can learn to read and write you have to know your ABCs. The Chinese have a different system. They do not use letters in an alphabet, but "characters" instead, like those being drawn on the opposite page. Each character represents a word or an idea. The Chinese language has more than 40,000 different characters. Each one is made up of a number of brush strokes that have to be drawn in a particular order. The rows of characters are written from top to bottom, rather than from left to right. The earliest known Chinese writing dates to the Shang **dynasty** more than 3,000 years ago. Bronze objects used in their religious rituals were inscribed with characters. Written sentences from the Shang era have also been found on tortoise shells and animal bones. These are known as **oracle** bones.

Making Paper

A major breakthrough took place in the year AD 105: The Chinese found a way to make paper. A civil servant named Cai Lun boiled together silk scraps, tree bark, and bamboo in water, then pounded the mixture into a pulp. He spread the pulp on a screen and let the water drain from it. After he rolled it flat, a sheet of paper remained. The paper was then hung on a wall to dry *(left)*.

Would **You** *Believe?*

Fear of Books

A scholar pleads to stop Shi-huangdi from burning books outside the palace gates *(right)*. The emperor banned books that compared his cruel laws with the ways of the past.

Hidden Messages

When one ancient Shang king needed hunting advice, he turned to a diviner, who could predict the future or interpret hidden meanings. He wrote a secret message about hunting on the front of the bone and applied a heated iron rod to the back of the same bone *(above),* causing it to crack. The cracks on the "oracle bone" were then interpreted by the diviner. From these simple marks, diviners developed the first written words.

What Is Calligraphy?

Calligraphy, or beautiful handwriting, was one of the highest art forms in China. It was considered as much an art as painting, poetry, and music were. Ancient calligraphers used animal-hair brushes bundled with silk threads and glued into the hollow end of bamboo sticks.

Bamboo Strips

Before paper was invented, the Chinese wrote on thin strips of bamboo that they tied together. They kept government records on these strips, many of which still survive. The first Chinese books were also written on bamboo. These books were awkward to use and difficult to store, as they took up so much space.

Development of Characters

The symbols below show how the Chinese character "tiger" has changed over many years.

At first, the Chinese used a simple picture to represent the tiger. Then they included other information—for instance, how the character should be pronounced. Throughout all the changes, one thing remained—the tiger's tail.

Building on a Grand Scale

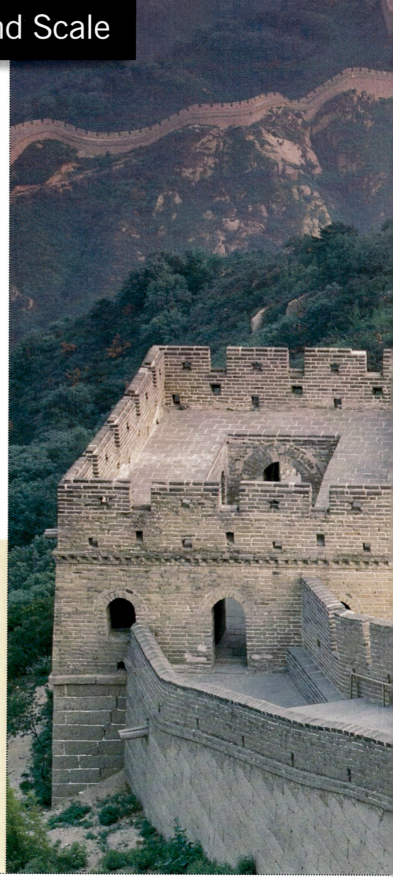

Nomadic horsemen roaming the land north of China often invaded the country and attacked Chinese villages. The First Emperor, Shihuangdi, was determined to stop the raiding. He sent 300,000 men—soldiers, farmers, and prisoners—north to build a long wall and guard the border. The workers joined together old sections of

walls, built since earliest times, and added on vast stretches of new ones. It was hard work far out on the frontier. Thousands died from exhaustion or starvation. Others tried to run away. Overseers hunted them down and killed them. So many bodies were buried in the earthen wall that it has been called the largest graveyard in the world. The First Emperor did not stop there. He had canals and roads built to connect the far corners of the country, which strengthened his control over China.

Fast FACTS

How long? No one knows exactly how long the twisting wall is, but it extends at least 2,500 km (1,500 mi.)—roughly the distance from New York City to Dallas, Texas.

How high? On average the Great Wall is 8 m (25 ft.) high, but some sections rise to 12 m (40 ft.)—the size of a four-story building. Ten soldiers could march side by side on top of the wall in its widest areas, and messengers rode along on horseback.

How many? As many as 25,000 watchtowers have been built, roughly one every 100 m (300 ft.).

How long did it take to build? The wall was built, and rebuilt, and added to over the course of 2,000 years.

What's it made of? The earliest walls were simple ones made of earth, twigs, clay, and gravel. The later walls were solid ones built of stone and brick.

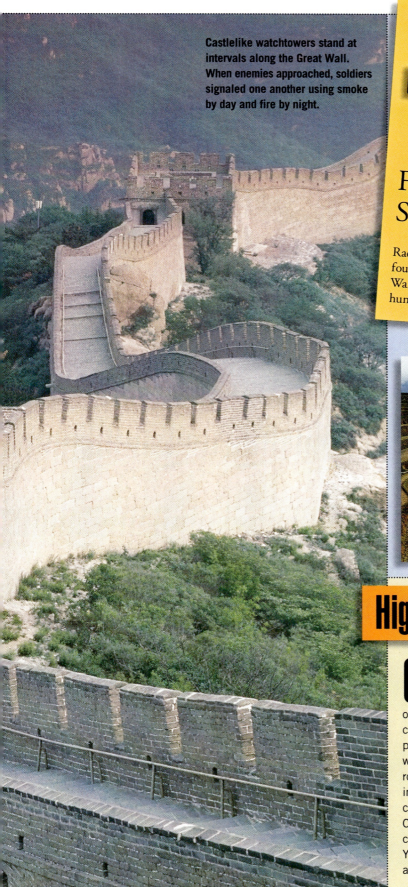

Castlelike watchtowers stand at intervals along the Great Wall. When enemies approached, soldiers signaled one another using smoke by day and fire by night.

Found from Space

Radar aboard the space shuttle found sections of the Great Wall that are invisible to the human eye today. The orange line in this radar image is a 600-year-old portion of the wall. The broken green line beneath it is an older version that was built 1,500 years ago. Much of these walls had been buried under desert sand. The radar could see through 6 m (20 ft.) of sand.

Terracing

Droughts often ruined China's crops, and much of the country seemed too mountainous to farm. In a clever solution, farmers cut flat, narrow fields (like the rice fields at left) into hillsides. This method, called terracing, saved water and made use of every bit of land.

Highways of Water

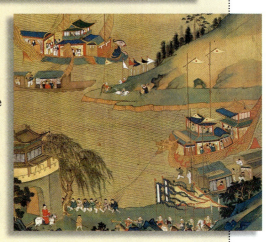

Chinese emperors ordered canals built to connect rivers to different parts of the country. These waterways served as early roads. The canals built in ancient times led to construction of the Grand Canal (right), a project connecting the Yangzi and Yellow Rivers, in the sixth and seventh **centuries.**

The Silk Road

The Production of Silk

In 139 BC the emperor sent an official named Zhang Qian west into central Asia to get help against northern invaders, but his attempts failed. On his return, Zhang Qian told of splendid horses for sale in central Asia. These would be useful in fighting the northerners. In exchange, the Chinese could trade their most precious product—silk. The luxurious fabric was unknown anywhere else and could be sold at a high price. One roll of silk was worth nearly 360 kg (800 lb.) of rice. Thus began the Silk Road—the trade route from China to the Mediterranean, through some of the most inhospitable regions in the world: snow-topped mountains and deserts like the Taklamakan, which the Chinese called the "sea of death," with dunes up to 100 m (300 ft.) high. Camel caravans traveled for months to cross the thousands of miles.

Mediterranean Sea
Taklamakan Desert
Samarkand — Loulan
Kashi
Antioch — Baghdad
Silk Road — Chang'an
CHINA
INDIA
INDIAN OCEAN

Women's Work

According to an old Chinese saying, "Men plow and women weave." Women managed every aspect of silk making, from raising the silkworms to spinning the fine thread and weaving the cloth on a loom. Here, women iron a roll of finished cloth by stretching the fabric and pressing it with a heated pan.

Step One

Soft silk is actually made by an insect. The thread is spun by the caterpillar of a moth—the so-called silkworm. Workers at left fill baskets with the silkworm's favorite food, leaves from the mulberry tree, a widely planted tree in China.

Step Two

Silkworms eat constantly and grow so fast that in about a month's time they shed their skin four times. The women at right feed them freshly chopped mulberry leaves up to 10 times a day. They also keep the sensitive silkworms warm.

Step Three

When it has grown fat, the silkworm releases a thread from an opening below its mouth and forms a cocoon. Before it turns into an adult moth and bursts through the cocoon —and breaks the continuous thread—a worker kills the developing moth over steam.

Step Four

Each cocoon is made up of one several-thousand-foot-long thread. A worker pulls out the delicate thread without breaking it and combines and twists the strands from seven cocoons to make one strong silk thread. The threads are later woven into silk fabric.

A Silkworm Smuggler

Only the Chinese knew how to make silk. People all over the world would pay a high price for it—and China wanted to keep it that way. Taking silkworm eggs out of the country was against the law and punishable by death. The fifth-**century** Chinese princess shown at left loved silk so much that she risked her life for it. She hid silkworms in her crown when she went off to marry a king in central Asia and gave away the secret.

Thousands for a Spool of Thread

How many silkworms do you need to make a pound of silk? It takes more than 2,000 silkworms to produce 1 pound of silk thread. Even today, silk is the most highly prized fabric, being soft and shimmering like the ancient silk garment above.

Monsters and Singing Sand

Chinese merchants crossed barren lands with heavily loaded camels to trade silk for horses from central Asia. Travelers were frightened by stories of monsters on the trail and hot winds that could destroy them. The "Singing Sand" mountain along the way *(above)* was said to thunder when disturbed.

Inventions and Discoveries

From the times of the earliest emperors, the Chinese invented amazing new ways of doing things. When they first had contact with foreigners, they believed that foreigners must be carefully watched, perhaps even feared, but that their ideas were not worth much. Chinese ways were best. During the time described in this book, the Chinese invented paper, the **compass,** and the seismograph, to detect earthquakes; they studied sunspots and manufactured steel in large quantities, long before anyone else. From steel, they made strong weapons and superior parts for farming equipment, plow tips, hoes, and wheelbarrows, which resulted in a dramatic increase in food production. Many Chinese ideas and innovations slowly made their way to India, the **Middle East,** and Europe by way of the Silk Road and were copied much later by the rest of the world.

Instruments of War

The invention of the crossbow *(above)* in the fourth century BC changed warfare for centuries. With the new Chinese weapon, arrows released by a trigger mechanism could be shot from a long distance. This eliminated the need for chariot raids. The use of metal stirrups *(left)* made mounting a horse and riding much easier. It also allowed men in heavy armor to stay on their horses, paving the way for heavily armed cavalry in the Middle Ages.

Farm Tools

Then & NOW!

The wheelbarrow was invented by the Chinese in the first **century** BC. Although today's wheelbarrow looks different, the principle has not changed. The Chinese called it a "wooden ox" or a "gliding horse." The West did not have wheelbarrows for another 1,300 years.

Irrigation

A simple chain pump invented in China in the first century AD is still used in modern China to irrigate fields. Balancing themselves on a wooden bar, Chinese farmers power the pump by stepping on a treadmill. An endless chain then draws wooden pallets holding water up through a chute to reach the field. Water from a stream or **irrigation** ditch can be raised as high as 4.5 m (15 ft.) with these pumps.

Navigation

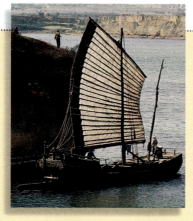

Christopher Columbus would never have made it to America without two Chinese inventions —the compass, for setting the right course, and the rudder, for steering the ship. In the fourth century BC the Chinese discovered that a lodestone, a mineral that acts like a magnet, could be used to indicate direction. They devised a simple compass, like the one below, which always aimed south. The spoon-shaped pointer in

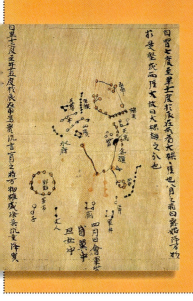

the center represents the constellation the Big Dipper.

Wooden rudders, invented in China in the first century AD, were hinged to the back of a ship below the waterline and could swing left and right. When a sailor turned the rudder, it created enough water resistance to change the boat's direction. Above, a modern Chinese sailboat built to an ancient design, called a junk, is controlled by this kind of rudder, which is partly visible above the water. Both compasses and rudders came to the rest of the world only in the 12th century.

Charting the Heavens

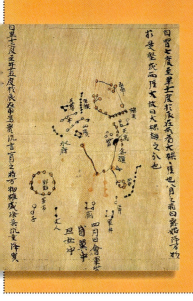

Ancient Chinese astronomers studied the heavens and kept records of everything they saw. The chart at left, grouping stars into constellations, was based on the observations of fourth-century BC astronomers. Emperors were fearful of bad omens from the heavens. When in 211 BC a large meteorite fell on China, the emperor ordered the meteorite destroyed and put to death everyone living near where it fell. The Chinese believed that the emperor was the Son of Heaven. Unusual celestial events should be predicted by the emperor and his astronomers. If he could not, it showed that the emperor was no longer fit to rule.

Medical Discoveries

Feeling seasick? A traditional Chinese doctor would insert sharp needles just above your right wrist. This form of medicine, known as **acupuncture,** was used as early as 1500 BC. The Chinese believe the body has a natural balance; when that balance is disturbed, illness results. Energy in the body flows along 14 lines, each linked to a different organ or function. The ancient chart at

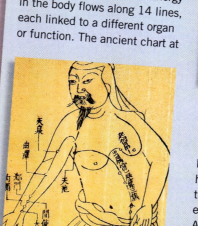

left shows specific needle points on the circulation line running along the right arm.

By the second century BC, the Chinese understood how blood circulates through the body (an idea unknown elsewhere until the 16th century AD). The Chinese doctor above takes his patient's pulse while an assistant stands ready with needles.

Everyday Objects

When it rains what do you reach for? Your umbrella, of course— another Chinese invention. The umbrella was created in the fourth century and was first made of heavy oiled paper produced from mulberry tree bark. Only the emperor could use red or yellow umbrellas; ordinary people carried blue ones.

Religion The Three Ways

For nearly 2,000 years there have been three main religions, or "three ways" of thought, in China: Confucianism, Daoism, and Buddhism. All offer different ways to achieve harmony, which the Chinese believe is the greatest virtue. Confucianism teaches that following a code of proper behavior will lead to peace and favors an organized government. Followers of Daoism believe that man-made governments and laws interfere with the natural order. People should follow nature's way, or "Dao." Buddhism teaches that giving up worldly desires can lead to "enlightenment." These religions differ, but the Chinese have an old saying: "The three teachings flow into one." The Chinese have developed a rich mixture of beliefs that includes elements of all "three ways," although most go to Buddhist temples to worship.

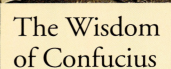

What Is Yin/Yang?

The symbol above represents yin and yang—the ancient Chinese belief that the world is a harmonious mixture of all things. The dark, yin part of the circle represents the earthly, female, and wet elements of nature; the light, yang portion stands for the heavenly, male, and dry elements. The opposing forces balance each other.

The Wisdom of Confucius

Confucius, China's best-known thinker, was born in 551 BC during a period of warfare. He preached that everyone must know his proper role in life. Children must honor and obey their parents, as shown in the scene below. This was known as filial piety. The same respect must be shown toward others in authority.

Daoism

Fanciful Gods

The fierce-looking figure at left was a popular Daoist god who protected households from evil. On New Year's Day his picture would be hung on the front door to ensure blessings for the coming year. Daoists worshiped many gods who were both serious and playful—like elves in fairy tales. The eight "immortals" had discovered the key to living forever. They lived in the mountains and had magical powers such as making themselves invisible, changing objects into gold, and forcing flowers to bloom instantly.

The Old Master

Lao Zi, the legendary founder of Daoism, is often shown riding on the back of a water buffalo (below) to represent his closeness with nature. Born around the same time as Confucius, Lao Zi taught that people are part of nature and should live in perfect harmony with it. Everything in life should be done in accordance with nature's rhythms—even daily physical exercise. Daoists closely studied the way animals move when they fight, and then developed shadowboxing exercises based on their movements. Throughout China, groups of shadowboxers can still be seen in parks doing their morning exercises.

Buddhism

Merchants traveling along the Silk Road brought exotic spices and gold to China. In the first **century** AD they also imported a religion from India called Buddhism (pages 50-51). Buddhism was based on the teachings of the Buddha, a prince from northern India. After the religion spread to China, local monks began carving enormous stone Buddhas, like the one above, out of rock walls. Typically, the Buddha's face would not show any emotion—as if he were meditating. On one Chinese cliff that stretched for more than half a mile, 51,000 Buddhist images were carved, inviting **meditation.**

Social Scene

Social Order

Ancient Chinese society was divided into several levels according to Confucian ideals. The emperor and the royal family were far above everyone else. The emperor was considered to be on the same level as a god, for he was believed to have direct authority from heaven. On the second-highest level were government officials trained in Confucian ideas. They made decisions on governing the country and served the royal family. Below them were farmers. Although farmers were usually poor, working the soil was considered a noble profession. Next on the social ladder were **artisans,** who made useful items such as clothing and furniture. The lowest ones were the merchants. They were looked down upon for growing rich by trading while producing nothing with their own hands. They led far easier lives than peasants or artisans but earned envy rather than true respect.

1 Emperor's Family

Ladies of the court, like these members of the royal family, were surrounded by luxury. They spent their time entertaining and taking part in official ceremonies.

2 Officials

China was vast and required a huge number of government workers to keep things orderly. Officials—unlike most people —could read and write. They registered births and deaths, collected taxes, enforced laws, and organized building projects. As early as 124 BC, unusually bright boys could hope to be sent to an imperial academy, to study the writings of Confucius. In later years students had to pass difficult tests that lasted for days. If they passed the examinations, they won a job as an official and the respect of their community.

3 Farmers

"Agriculture is the foundation of the world," a Chinese emperor said. Most Chinese were farmers who worked small pieces of land, doing everything by hand. Farmers along the Yellow River in northern China mainly grew wheat, barley, and **millet.** The soil was rich, but farmers often suffered through both droughts and floods. The Yellow River flooded so often, it was called China's Sorrow. When water rose too high, the farmers would build barriers to try to prevent flooding *(above)*.

Houses

Chinese families needed large houses. Grandparents, aunts and uncles, parents and children all lived together—and they might not all get along. To create pockets of privacy, the Chinese built houses around courtyards, with different branches of the family living in separate courtyards. The main house for well-to-do Chinese was often several stories high,

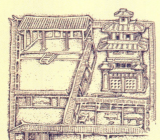

like the one above. Inside the doorway to the house was a "spirit screen" that blocked any view of the inner courtyard. The Chinese believed that this kept evil spirits—which move only in straight lines—out of the house.

4

Artisans

Chinese artisans worked hard—they never had a day off except for three days for the New Year celebration and the day they married. They produced weapons and cookware, as well as beautiful objects of bronze or jade, pieces of pottery, and fine furniture. As payment, they received food and clothing, or money. Artisans skilled at a particular craft usually worked together in groups under the direction of a master, like these carpenters at right. They labored in factories usually run by the government.

5

Merchants

With the wealth created by the Silk Road trade, bustling city streets *(below)* were filled with shops of every kind. The Chinese loved the strange new products they could buy, but they resented rich merchants. During the Han **dynasty,** laws were passed to shame them. They were not allowed to ride on horseback or to wear silk clothing. Instead, they had to wear a special white turban so that everyone would know who they were.

Fun & Games

Musical Harmony

The ancient Chinese liked to have fun and especially enjoyed theater, dance, and music. The words "music" and "enjoyment" both use the same character, which led a Confucian thinker to say, "Music is joy." Since ancient times the Chinese have celebrated festivals that are still observed today. Some are based on the cycles of the moon. On one night in September when the Chinese believe the moon shines brightest, families gather for dinner and eat piles of round, sweet moon cakes. The Dragon Boat Festival in late May or early June honors the poet Qu Yuan, who drowned himself more than 2,000 years ago when he was unable to change a corrupt government. While looking for Qu Yuan, the searchers threw rice in the water, hoping hungry fish would eat the rice instead of the body. The festival is marked by boat races and the eating of sweet rice dumplings—reminders of the searchers' desperate hunt for the poet and the rice they tossed to the fish.

Would You Believe?

Killer Kites

Can you imagine never having seen a kite before? Do you think you'd be frightened the first time you saw one? The enemies of the Chinese did get scared. When the Chinese invented kites, during the Han **dynasty,** the army sometimes used them to startle their enemies. Kites had a more peaceful use as well—early Daoists meditated as they flew kites. They were also said to ride the "hard wind" on kitelike structures. Imagine that—hang gliding back in the fourth **century** BC.

To Confucius, music was almost as important as food. "It soothes the soul," he said. "It is the harmony of Heaven and earth." But people also said that the wrong kind of music could lead to wild behavior. The courts of Chinese emperors resounded with music. Women at court played several instruments, including the classical lute *(above, right).* During religious rituals men struck bells with hammers and canes. The bells at top are part of a 64-bell set discovered in the tomb of a ruler from 433 BC. He so loved music that he was buried with 124 instruments, as well as 21 young musicians.

Entertainment

Comic actors, musicians, and acrobats traveled from town to town making people laugh and forget their day-to-day struggles. People invited entertainers to their home to amuse their guests. These performers were so beloved that some Chinese wanted to take them along to the afterlife. Miniature clay statues like the ones above and below were placed in ancient tombs. These figures capture the energy of the performers. They would do anything to make their audience laugh or surprise them with their stunts. The actor above kicks up his leg while banging on a drum under his arm. The drummer at left is about to lose his pants but keeps on clanging.

Happy New Year!

On New Year's Day all of China bursts into celebration. In ancient times the party lasted for 15 days! Even now, during that time the Chinese visit with family and friends, exchange gifts, sweep their houses to begin the year with a fresh start, and enjoy lion and dragon dancers (above) parading through town.

Phoenicians People at the Crossroads

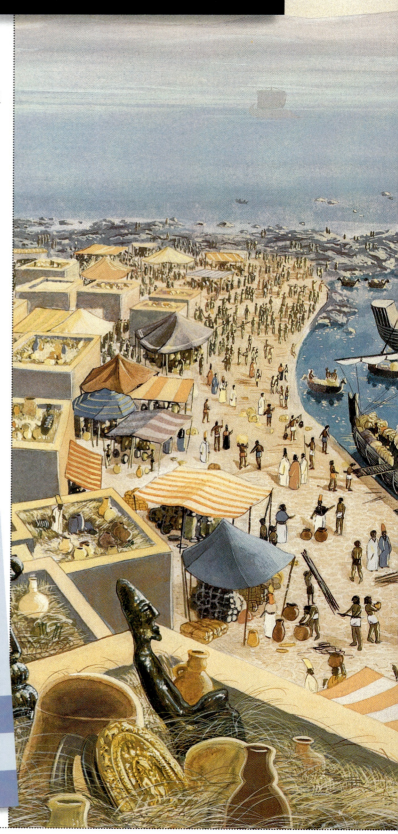

Until about 2000 BC the major **civilizations** —Mesopotamia, Egypt, India, and China— had developed along river valleys and existed fairly isolated from one another. As these societies grew, they began to spill over into other peoples' lands. A great meeting place between Egypt and Mesopotamia was the narrow strip of land between the Mediterranean Sea and the cedar-covered mountains of Lebanon. Among the region's earliest settlers were the Phoenicians, who established small **city-states** along the coast. From their coastal cities of Byblos, Sidon, and Tyre, they sailed sturdy boats —built with their mountain cedars— throughout the Mediterranean. They founded trading posts and colonies in North Africa and as far away as present-day Spain. Besides trade goods, they distributed knowledge from the many foreign cultures they had contact with and helped spread the ideas of civilization.

The First Alphabet

The Phoenicians found Egyptian-style picture writing to be ill suited for recordkeeping. So they developed a word-based writing system using 22 symbols—the forerunner of our alphabet.

Sign	Name	Meaning	Letter
Ḵ	Aleph	Ox	A
◁	Beth	House	B
⌐	Gimel	Camel	C, G
◿	Daleth	Door	D

The Polestar

The Phoenicians noticed that the polestar (or North Star) is the only star that remains in the same spot all night long. Great navigators that they were, they used this knowledge for sailing. Instead of having to rely on shore-based landmarks to fix their position, they could keep the polestar in their sights to calculate distances far out at sea.

Byblos

The Phoenician city of Byblos was an important trading center. From there cedar trees were shipped as far as Egypt in exchange for **papyrus.** This papyrus-cedar exchange in Byblos happened so regularly that the name Byblos was adopted by the Greeks as the word for "book" and gave us the English word "Bible."

Tyrian Purple

The port city of Tyre was famous for its dyed cloth, especially in the color known as Tyrian purple. The dye came from a small gland in the body of the murex snail *(below).* It took 60,000 snails to produce 1 pound of the precious dye. At today's prices, 1 pound of the dye would cost thousands of dollars! Because of the terrible smell from rotting snails, the dye works were located downwind of the city. On the outskirts of Tyre you can still see huge mounds containing millions of murex shells marking the remains of this ancient industry.

The Kingdom of Israel

We know more about ancient Israel than about many other cultures of that time because the people and their traditions still survive. According to Jewish scripture, Israel's history began with the prophet Abraham, who led his people, the Semites, out of Mesopotamia to the land of Canaan, where the Phoenicians *(pages 70-71)* lived as well. There was friction between these newcomers and the Canaanites over land and religious beliefs. Like all other cultures then, the Canaanites worshiped many gods, but Abraham's followers had only Yahweh. They were the first people to practice **monotheism.** In their long and turbulent history they were often persecuted and sometimes enslaved for their different beliefs. For several **centuries** the tribes of Israel were loosely grouped and ruled by judges. In about 1020 BC, in a fight to rout invaders, a local judge named Saul united the tribes and established the kingdom of Israel.

Tablets of the Law

In the Old Testament story of the Israelites' escape from Egypt, Moses led his people into the Sinai Desert; they wandered there for 40 years before being allowed to enter the "Promised Land." While in the desert, Moses received a message from God, promising that He would protect His "chosen people." In return the Israelites would worship only one God and follow His laws—the Ten Commandments, contained on two stone tablets *(left).*

Would **You** *Believe?*

The Torah

The holy book of the Jews is called the Torah. The text is the same as the first five chapters of the Bible. Written by hand on a long scroll of parchment, the Torah contains the history of the ancient Israelites and the laws handed down by God that the Jews must follow in their daily lives.

From Friend to Foe

Israelites first entered Egypt as traders, such as this traveling group of metalworkers shown in a painting from an Egyptian tomb. At first they were well received. Many eventually settled in Egypt, but later **pharaohs** took a different view of these foreigners and reduced them to the status of slaves. Moses led their flight from Egypt back to the land of Canaan.

Passover Celebration

During Passover, which celebrates the Israelites' flight from Egypt, Jewish families gather for a service called the seder. Each member plays a role and recites lines in the story of the **Exodus.** Every item on the seder table represents a part of the tale: Bitter herbs recall the pain of slavery, unleavened bread reflects the Israelites' hurried flight (they had no time to let the bread rise), four cups of wine signify the four promises God made to His "chosen people."

According to legend, a young Israelite boy killed a fearsome Philistine warrior, named Goliath, with only a sling and a pebble. The boy, David, was hailed as a hero by his people and later became King Saul's son-in-law and the greatest king of Israel. In about 1000 BC, David made Jerusalem his capital. During his 40-year reign, Israel fought and won many wars, growing in size and power. David's son, Solomon, proved as skillful in **diplomacy** as his father had been in battle. He signed peace treaties with neighboring countries that guaranteed Israel's security. After Solomon's death, the country split into the kingdoms of Israel and Judah. Their rivalry prompted many wars, and their power declined. Conqueror followed conqueror: the Persians, Greeks, and Romans. In the year AD 1 under the Roman emperor Augustus, Jesus was born in Bethlehem. His birth led to a new religion, which we know as Christianity. But the Jewish faith survives to this day.

King Solomon

Solomon was respected as a fair king and a wise judge. In the medieval illustration above he is shown unfurling a scroll of laws. According to the Scriptures, when God appeared to him in a dream to grant him one request, Solomon asked for wisdom. In one trial famous for his wise judgment, an infant was brought before him by two women, each claiming to be its mother. Solomon picked up a sword and said that he would cut the baby in two, giving one half to each woman. At this, one of them begged him not to harm the child but to give it to the other woman, proving that she must be the real mother.

Dome of the Rock

A rock outcrop on Jerusalem's Temple Mount is said by Jews and Christians to mark the spot where Abraham prepared to sacrifice his son to God. Muslims believe the prophet Mohammed ascended to heaven from the same spot. A seventh-**century mosque** now encloses this site, which is sacred to all three religions.

The Wailing Wall

One of Solomon's great achievements was the building of a magnificent temple on a hill in Jerusalem known as the Temple Mount. Nothing is left of the temple today except for a portion of the wall that supported its base. Known as the Western (or Wailing) Wall, it is the holiest site in all of Judaism. Jews from all over the world travel there to pray on behalf of departed relatives, often leaving prayers on folded paper in the cracks between the stones, because "the Divine Presence never moves, which was not destroyed and never will be destroyed."

Jerusalem

In this model of the ancient city, Solomon's Second Temple rises behind the fortress walls on the Temple Mount. The Babylonians had destroyed the First Temple in 587 BC and driven out the Israelites, who, returning 50 years later, rebuilt the Temple on the same spot. It, too, was razed, by the Romans in AD 70. A second Roman suppression followed in AD 135. Israel would not regain its independence until it was rebuilt as the modern nation-state in 1948.

Court Life

During the time when Israelite kings ruled Jerusalem, life at court was an elegant affair. This ivory carving shows a royal deputy and a musician attending to the king while a soldier stands guard.

The Dead Sea Scrolls

In 1947, two shepherd boys discovered some clay jars in a cave overlooking the Dead Sea. The jars contained several parchment scrolls—the one shown below is 8.2 m (27 ft.) long—covered with ancient writing. They turned out to be one of the greatest archaeological discoveries of all time. The nearly-1,900-year-old scrolls contained the earliest known version of several books of the Torah.

Lost World of the Minoans

Palace of Knossos

Sprawled across 20,000 sq. m (5 acres), the Palace of Knossos rose in many tiers, with colonnaded halls, grand staircases, and hundreds of rooms. Archaeologists believe this palace and its surrounding buildings may have supported 30,000 people. Among its conveniences were running water, bathtubs, and toilets.

The first **civilization** to emerge in the eastern Mediterranean developed on the island of Crete, south of mainland Greece. The islanders, called Minoans after the legendary king Minos, lived a life centered on the sea. They built sturdy boats and became fishermen and sailors. About 2000 BC, they began building large palaces that served as administrative centers for their trade with the Egyptians, the Mesopotamians, and the Phoenicians. Palaces had storerooms for grain and the olive oil and wine produced on Crete alongside workshops where skilled craftsmen made pottery. Sometime after 1450 BC, the lively Minoans mysteriously disappeared. Many **archaeologists** believe that a volcanic eruption on the nearby island of Thera may have caused destruction on Crete as well and left the island open to invasion.

GREECE

THERA

CRETE

Mediterranean Sea

Ladies of the Court

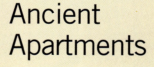

Their long hair styled in perfect curls and festooned with jewels, three ladies watch a public event from a grandstand, in the **fresco** above. Minoans took great care about their looks: Archaeologists found beauty aids such as mirrors, combs, and cosmetics cases.

Ancient Apartments

Not all Minoans lived in lavish palaces. The models below, which resemble modern townhouses, show how ordinary people lived in the cities that surrounded the palaces. The ground floor of a small house was used for storage and cooking. Bedrooms were located on the upper floors. Open skylights on the roof kept the rooms light and airy. Any rain that fell through the skylights was collected in large pots for household use.

A Link to the Sea

Minoan potters revealed their love for the sea in designs like the wriggling octopus on the jar at right. Their pottery was famous for its fine craftsmanship. Similar storage jars, used for holding oil, grain, and olives, have been found in cities all around the Mediterranean. These finds are evidence of the Minoans' far-flung trade.

Imagine That!

A Labyrinth

The many rooms and twisted corridors of the Palace of Knossos may have inspired the legend of the **Minotaur.** A terrifying creature—half man, half bull—the minotaur was said to prowl a maze-like **labyrinth** beneath the palace, commemorated on the ancient coin below. Once inside the labyrinth, no one could find a way out.

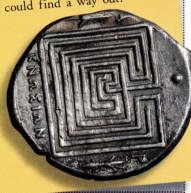

Would You Believe?

Bull Leaping

A skilled acrobat somersaults over the back of a bull in the fresco at right. Bulls were sacred to the Minoans, and bull leaping was probably a daring form of religious ritual.

Who Were the Mycenaeans?

Between 1600 and 1100 BC the Mycenaeans dominated mainland Greece. Named for the city where their **civilization** was first discovered, the Mycenaeans lived in scattered kingdoms around Greece. They spoke an early form of Greek and shared common religious beliefs.

Mycenaeans built their cities on high ground, called the acropolis, surrounded by protective walls. The palace served as the administrative center for the government and as a military headquarters. Like the Minoans, the Mycenaeans traded with lands all around the eastern Mediterranean.

The *Iliad* and the *Odyssey* tell how these early Greeks, led by King Agamemnon, fought in the war against Troy on the coast of what is now Turkey. For 10 years the Greeks laid siege to the heavily defended city. They sought to reclaim Helen, the Greek princess who had been carried off by Paris, a Trojan prince. The stories of this bloody war and the Greek victory live on today.

MACEDONIA
Mt. Olympus
Troy
Ithaca
Athens
Mycenae
CRETE
Mediterranean Sea

People — Heinrich Schliemann

Heinrich Schliemann, a German businessman, believed the stories told in Homer's *Iliad* and *Odyssey* were true. In 1870, he used clues from the poems to find the city of Troy and **excavate** much of its buried treasure. Years later he also found Mycenae.

Trojan War

Trick Horse

After 10 years of war against the Trojans, the Greeks simply sailed away, leaving a large wooden horse *(left)* at the city gates of Troy. When the Trojans dragged their gift inside for a closer look, Greek warriors poured out and took up the fight. Aided by the returning army, the Greeks defeated Troy and won the war.

Death Mask

This gold burial mask from a Mycenaean tomb probably belonged to a king. Heinrich Schliemann *(below, left)* thought it depicted King Agamemnon, the leader of the Greeks against Troy, but **archaeologists** have dated it to an earlier time.

Homer

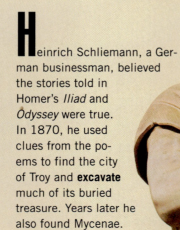

Homer *(left)* was a blind poet who lived in about 750 BC. He retold the legends of the Trojan War hundreds of years after it occurred in two **epics,** the *Iliad* and the *Odyssey*. His performances were an early form of theater: To the beat of drums or music, he recited his poems for hours. To tell one story from beginning to end would have taken more than 10 hours!

Armor

Archaeologists discovered this bronze suit of armor and wild-boar-tusk helmet in a soldier's grave. Weapons and armor found in their graves suggest that Mycenaeans were often at war. Homer called the Mycenaean warriors "the strongest generation of earth-born mortals."

Linear B

Mycenaeans kept records in an early form of Greek writing called Linear B. Archaeologists have found hundreds of tablets like the one shown here, which contained detailed lists of palace inventories, religious offerings, and administrative statistics. One careful **scribe** even recorded the names of two cows—Blackie and Glossie!

Lion Gate

Two stone lions, each 3.5 m (10 ft.) tall, guarded the main entrance to Mycenae. Behind them, 7-m (20-ft.)-thick walls encircled the city to protect it from invaders. Later generations of Greeks called the walls cyclopean. They believed that only mythical giants, like the one-eyed **Cyclops**, could have moved stones so large.

Greece The Rise of City-States

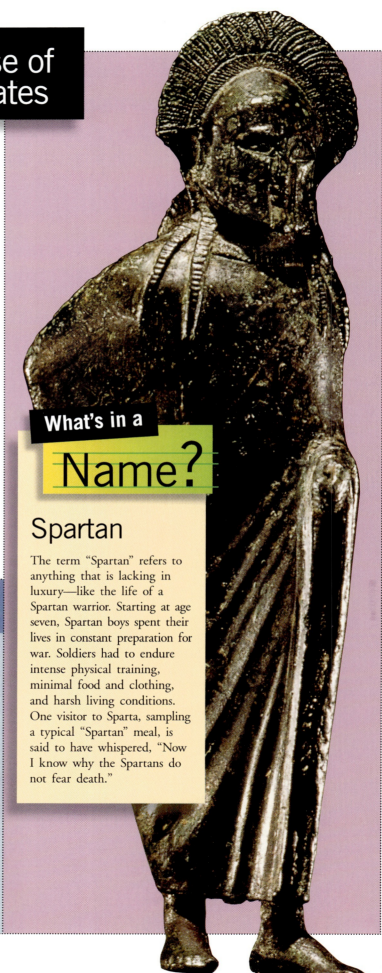

During the eighth **century** BC, almost 300 years after the decline of the Mycenaean **civilization,** Greece entered a new period of prosperity. Trade increased, the population grew, and large **city-states** began to form. Each city-state, or polis, consisted of a walled city, with a marketplace and acropolis at its center, and surrounding farmland. Several hundred city-states, among them Sparta, Athens, Thebes, and Corinth, spread across the mountainous terrain of Greece and the surrounding islands. Each state had its own government and **patron** god or goddess. Only men who owned land could hold citizenship in the polis. Citizens had to serve in the army and participate in the city council. One of the first city-states was Sparta, founded in Greece about 900 BC. After suffering several crushing military defeats, Sparta devoted itself to training for war; it developed little art or culture. By contrast, Athens, the largest city-state, became a center for culture, learning, and trade.

Fighting in a Phalanx

Marching in tight formation to the tune of a flute, a Greek phalanx attacks the enemy in the illustration below. A phalanx consisted of rows of soldiers marching close together, so that each man's shield also protected his neighbor. Sparta perfected the use of the phalanx. By the sixth century BC, it had the strongest fighting force in Greece.

What's in a Name?

Spartan

The term "Spartan" refers to anything that is lacking in luxury—like the life of a Spartan warrior. Starting at age seven, Spartan boys spent their lives in constant preparation for war. Soldiers had to endure intense physical training, minimal food and clothing, and harsh living conditions. One visitor to Sparta, sampling a typical "Spartan" meal, is said to have whispered, "Now I know why the Spartans do not fear death."

The Temples on the Acropolis

Rising 70 m (200 ft.) above the city, the ruins of Athens's Acropolis give but a hint of what was once its spiritual center, with the Parthenon at right and the Erechtheion below.

Cool Columns

Caryatid columns, modeled after women from the island of Caria, support the roof of the Erechtheion. A small temple dedicated to the goddess Athena *(inset and to the left of the Parthenon),* it marked the legendary site of Athens's first olive tree, a symbol of the city's prosperity.

Would You Believe?

Not a Single Straight Line!

Greek architects knew that straight lines on large buildings cause an optical illusion that makes them look as if they dip or sag in the middle. To correct the problem, they designed the columns of the Parthenon to bulge slightly in the center, taper at the top, and lean into the building. They also raised the floor and the ceiling slightly in the middle. Called refinements, these carefully calculated curves help draw the eye up, enhancing the building's height. The Parthenon is considered a marvel of both architecture and science; its style has been copied for more than 2,000 years.

People

Pericles

Pericles was the leader of Athens during its golden age—a period of about 50 years following Greece's victory over the Persians in 479 BC. In celebration Pericles ordered the construction of new public buildings and temples, including the Parthenon. He wanted Athens to be the most beautiful city on earth. In a speech he boasted that "future generations will wonder at us, as the present age wonders at us now."

Gods of Mount Olympus

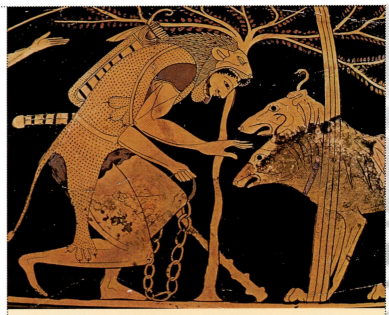

The cloud-covered peak of Mount Olympus was home to the Olympians, the gods and goddesses of the Greek world. Ruled by Zeus, the 12 Olympians looked like humans but were immortal—they could never die. The Greeks believed that the gods were always watching them and had powers to cause both good and bad things in their lives. Most houses had small shrines, where Greeks worshiped almost daily. They prayed to Aphrodite, the goddess of love, and to Demeter, who had the power to help crops grow strong and tall. They feared Poseidon, who with a touch of his **trident** could cause the earth to tremble or stir up a violent storm at sea. The Greeks went to great lengths to please the gods. They built beautiful temples and offered animal **sacrifices** to win the gods' favor. They also organized processions, staged plays, and competed in athletic festivals in their gods' honor.

The Story of Herakles

Herakles (the Roman Hercules) was famous for his strength. The son of Zeus and a mortal queen, he was given 12 seemingly impossible tasks to atone for murders he committed while under a spell. His tasks included killing the Hydra, a snake with many heads, and strangling a lion. Above, Herakles captures Cerberus, the three-headed guardian dog of the underworld. When he completed his 12 labors, Herakles became an immortal.

Home of the Gods

mysterious mist. Ancient Greeks believed this was the home of the gods.

Mount Olympus

Mount Olympus rises to 2,900 m (9,500 ft.) and is the highest mountain on mainland Greece. Its peak is often hidden by a

The omphalos, a stone in a temple in Delphi, was said to be the navel of the world. At this ancient religious site high in the mountains, foul-smelling fumes rose from a crack in the earth. When priestesses breathed in the fumes and smoke from burning laurel leaves, they began to see visions of the future. Many people came to hear their predictions, called **oracles.**

Temple of Artemis at Ephesus

A forest of 127 gleaming marble columns supported the Temple of Artemis at Ephesus in one of the Greek colonies on the coast of modern Turkey. It was one of the largest Greek temples and counted among the **Seven Wonders of the World.**

The Underworld

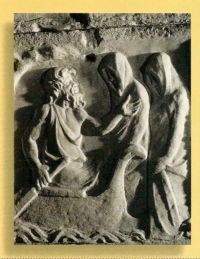

Greeks were buried with coins in their hands, to pay the ferryman Charon *(right)* for passage across the River Styx to the underworld. If they had led virtuous lives, they believed the ferryman would bring them to the Elysian Fields, a place of everlasting happiness. Wicked people would be condemned to Tartarus, a hellish place in the underworld, where they would suffer eternal punishment. The underworld was ruled by Hades, the god of the dead.

1. **Ares**—God of war
2. **Aphrodite**—Goddess of love and beauty
3. **Hermes**—Messenger of the gods and protector of travelers
4. **Hestia**—Goddess of the family and the hearth
5. **Poseidon**—God of earthquakes, the sea, horses, and bulls
6. **Athena**—Goddess of wisdom, art, and war
7. **Zeus**—Chief god; god of the sky and thunder
8. **Hera**—Goddess of marriage and childbirth
9. **Apollo**—God of the sun, music, and poetry
10. **Artemis**—Goddess of the moon and hunting and protector of girls
11. **Hephaistos**—God of fire and blacksmiths
12. **Demeter**—Goddess of crops, especially grain

The Birth of Democracy

A t the dawn of the sixth **century** BC, Athenians introduced reforms that allowed all citizens, not just the upper class, to participate in government. They called their new system democracy, which means "rule by the people." This was totally new: Until then, only kings and some lesser rulers made decisions for their people.

Now, about 50,000 citizens, all free males who had been born in Athens, were eligible to attend the *ekklesia,* or assembly. In the ekklesia, citizens debated important issues and discussed new laws. They made decisions by holding a vote at the end of the debate. A minimum attendance of 6,000 citizens was required to hold a vote. If not enough voters were present, they sent out a special police force to round up more from the crowd in the marketplace. An elected council of 500 men called the *boule* decided on matters to be discussed in the ekklesia. The boule also administered the day-to-day affairs of the government. Athenian courts tested laws passed by the ekklesia. There were no lawyers; only citizens could speak in court. Juries of between 201 and 2,500 men listened to trials and voted with bronze ballots.

What's in a Name?

Ostracism

Once a year, Athenians had a chance to get rid of unpopular politicians through a vote of ostracism. Citizens etched the name of a politician they didn't like on a piece of pottery called an *ostrakon.* The one above shows the name of Themistokles, a worthy statesman who was nonetheless ostracized in 471 BC. Any man who received more than 6,000 ostraka was banished from Athens for 10 years.

Greek Ideal

U nder the watchful eye of their **patron** goddess, Athena, Athenian warriors cast their votes in the ekklesia *(below).* Greeks strove to honor their state by being good citizens. They served in the government and the army and conducted themselves with honesty and intelligence. This standard of excellence was called *arete,* which meant "goodness." The word "idiot" also comes from the Greek. It described an ignorant person who did not hold public office.

In Court

Water Clock

During a trial, one juror acted as judge, four volunteered to count votes, and one was assigned to work the water clock *(left)*. The water clock was designed to curb long-winded speakers and keep proceedings moving along briskly. Speakers had about six minutes to make their case, the time it took for water to flow from the top pot to the bottom one. In the assembly, boring speakers were often booed off the floor.

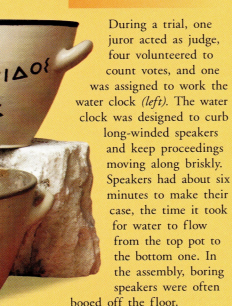

Jury Ballots

Jurors received two ballots at the beginning of a trial. They covered the center of the ballot with thumb and forefinger, so no one could see how they voted, and dropped it in a box. A ballot with a solid center was a vote for innocence; a hollow center meant guilty.

People

Solon

Solon was an elected leader of Athens in 594 BC at a time when only **aristocrats** had political power. He introduced reforms that allowed even the poorest citizens to participate in the assembly and has been called Father of Democracy.

Greek Legacy

Greek ideas have had a profound impact on governments throughout the world. In the United States in 1787 men in Philadelphia (the name comes from the Greek word for "brotherly love") drafted a Constitution based on the principles of Greek democracy. Many buildings in the city also reflect Greek influence in their design. The Philadelphia Art Museum *(below)* is a striking example of a modern building designed in the classic Greek style.

Let's Compare

Architectural Styles

Many public buildings and temples in ancient Greece were built in one of three styles, called orders. The easiest way to tell what order a building was built in is to examine the top of its columns. Doric columns are plain and square at the top. They are found on the earliest Greek buildings, including the Parthenon. The tops of Ionic columns are decorated with two swirls, called volutes. Buildings in the Ionic style are more delicate and open. A variation of Ionic columns, Corinthian columns have capitals, or tops, decorated with carved leaves.

Modern-day structures that are built in any of these orders are said to be built in the classical style.

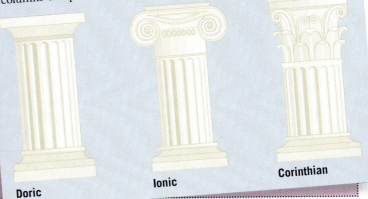

Doric   Ionic   Corinthian

Trade and Society

W hat could you find in an agora? Almost anything. The agora was a large, open marketplace in the center of a Greek city. Local grain, fish, meat, cheeses, and produce were for sale next to unusual spices, textiles, and perfumes from all over the world. Sandalmakers, potters, and other craftsmen operated tiny shops side by side in long halls called stoas that lined the square.

The agora was a sign of the lively trade between Greece, the islands and coastal stretches of the eastern Mediterranean settled by the Greeks, and foreign countries. By exporting olive oil, wine, pottery, and metal, Greek traders obtained grain and lumber and luxury items not easily found in their homeland. Trade allowed cities to grow beyond the natural limits of their food supply. Athens, for example, imported two-thirds of the grain it used.

Meet Me in the Agora

M eaning literally "gathering place," the agora was the heart of a Greek **city-state.** In ancient Athens *(above)* majestic government buildings, law courts, and temples lined the busy open marketplace. Men came to conduct business, discuss new ideas in the assembly, and catch up with friends. They also did the family shopping; it was not considered proper for free women to be seen there. Diversions abounded in the agora. Men could exercise at the nearby gymnasium or sit and watch the acrobats, musicians, and dancers who performed out in the open for spare coins.

Aristocrats

Greek society was a democracy, with rule by many citizens instead of by a single king, but not everybody was equal. At the top was a small group of wealthy citizens, **aristocrats,** like the well-dressed woman at left. They owned large tracts of land and had slaves to work for them. The government expected them to contribute to projects to benefit all and taxed them to pay for military expenses, such as building warships, and for arts festivals.

Farmers

Small farmers who owned land were also important members of the polis and were expected to participate in the city council after the harvest. Besides contributing to the food supply, they supported export trade with produce. The farmers shown on the vase at left are picking olives by shaking them off the tree's branches with poles. Olive oil was used in cooking, for burning in oil lamps, and for making soap.

Masters of the Sea

The mountainous terrain of Greece made travel by land slow and difficult. Greeks turned to the sea and built sturdy boats to carry them from port to port around the Mediterranean. The boat below is a replica of a **trireme**, or warship. It required 170 oarsmen to row it into battle.

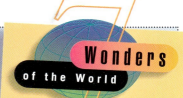
Colossus of Rhodes

A giant bronze statue of the sun god Helios stood near the harbor of Rhodes, an island near Turkey. Ancient historians claim that the Colossus stood more than 42 m (120 ft.) tall, unequaled for the times and said to be one of the **Seven Wonders.** It was toppled by an earthquake in 226 BC.

Metics

Many of the craftsmen and shopkeepers in the agora— like this barber—were metics. Metics were people who lived in a city-state but had not been born there, and so could not be considered citizens. About 10 percent, or 30,000, of the people living in Athens were metics. They could attend religious festivals and plays but were not permitted to vote or own property.

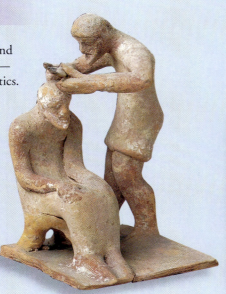

Slaves

Slaves usually came to Greece as prisoners of war. They made up about 25 percent of the population and did most of the heavy work. Their labor in fields and homes *(below)* allowed citizens free time to attend debates in the assembly.

Life at Home

For Greek women, life centered on the home. Most girls were married at age 14 or 15 to a much older man. Marriages were arranged by a girl's father. Often a bride met the groom for the first time on her wedding day. Once married, women took care of the household and raised children. They spent most of their days in the *gynaikeion,* the women's quarters of the house, which was quiet and far from the street. In the gynaikeion, women wove cloth for their family and entertained their friends. Women also cooked or supervised as slaves prepared family meals. Most families ate a basic meal of bread, fish, cheese, and fruit. On special occasions they dined on roasted songbirds, grasshoppers, snails, and other delicacies.

Although their husbands might hold important positions, women were not considered citizens. They could not own land or participate in the assembly. Only on rare occasions would they venture outside the house to go to the theater or a religious festival.

Greek Houses

A typical Greek house was built of mud brick and arranged around a central courtyard, like the model above. The courtyard had an altar for family worship and sometimes a small garden.

Houses had no running water, so slaves carried water from a well. Bedrooms were on the upper floor, together with the gynaikeion, where women spent their days. Rooms were sparsely furnished, with the exception of the dining room, where men held dinner parties. These rooms were lined with couches and had rugs or **mosaics** on the floor.

Wedding Party

On the day before her wedding, a bride left her toys at the Temple of Artemis to signify childhood's end. She bathed in sacred spring water and dressed in white. On the wedding night the groom arrived to claim his bride. A torchlight procession followed them to the groom's house, with well-wishers singing and throwing fruit and nuts to symbolize prosperity. Then the groom carried his bride over the threshold.

Party Games

*At a symposium, a fancy dinner party held for men, guests lay on couches and feasted on elaborate meals *(right)*. Slaves served the food and wine, and dancers, musicians, and acrobats provided after-dinner entertainment. Guests at a symposium also played games and told riddles, such as the examples at top right. See if you can guess what they describe. The answers are written upside down below.

When you look at me, I look at you, but I can't see you because I have no eyes. When you speak, I open my mouth and move my lips, but you cannot hear me because I have no voice. What am I?

What walks with four legs in the morning, two legs in the afternoon, and three legs at night?

Answers: 1. mirror 2. man as he grows from babyhood to old age

Guitar

Musicians often sang and strummed a kithara like the one below at religious festivals and special events. The instrument was an early form of the guitar, whose Greek name survives in our modern spelling. Greeks loved music and sang at every possible occasion. They had songs to celebrate the harvest and child-birth and even some to cure illness.

School attendance in Greece began at age seven. Boys usually studied with three different teachers. A *grammatistes* taught reading, writing, and math. Students learned to recite passages of Homer's poems the *Iliad* and the *Odyssey*. Memorizing these **epics** was meant to inspire students to emulate the heroes of Homer's classic tales. A *kitharistes* taught singing and playing the lyre and the flute. Musical skills were important at religious festivals and parties. The final part of a boy's education was athletics under a *paidotribes*. Boys practiced running, wrestling, and other sports that trained their bodies for athletic competition and for war. If girls received any formal education, it was in music and dancing. Their mothers taught them how to read and write.

Greek teachers and scholars discussed new ideas in the agora and attracted a large following of young people. Some of the great thinkers of the age are shown at right.

Pythagoras

Pythagoras discovered a formula for calculating the area of a right triangle *(left)* as $x^2+y^2=z^2$. He also used math to deduce that the earth revolves around the sun.

Hippocrates

Hippocrates encouraged doctors to use scientific methods to help cure patients. He studied how the body worked and the effect of different remedies. He is remembered today when new doctors swear the Hippocratic oath, promising to take care of patients to the best of their ability.

Socrates

The philosopher Socrates challenged people to think about their definitions of truth, good, and evil. His examinations often proved that people's beliefs were poorly thought out. Among his students were Plato and Aristotle, who later founded their own schools of philosophy.

Herodotus

Herodotus is often called the Father of History. In the fifth **century** BC he traveled to Egypt and Persia to collect stories for his *Histories,* an account of the Persian Wars with Greece, which was the starting point of Western history writing.

Greek Alphabet

The Greeks added vowel sounds to the older Phoenician characters *(page 70)* to derive their 24-letter alphabet. Several Greek letters, including alpha and beta (hence "alphabet"), are shown below. Students practiced writing these letters on a wax-covered tablet with a **stylus** *(right)*. The blunt end of the stylus acted as an eraser, allowing them to rub out mistakes.

A	Alpha	A	Z	Zeta	Z
B	Beta	B	K	Kappa	K
Γ	Gamma	G	Λ	Lambda	L
Δ	Delta	D	Π	Pi	P

Long Jump

Under the critical eye of his paidotribes *(above),* a student practices the standing long jump. Boys jumped over pits that varied in size according to their age. They released hand weights made of lead in midair to increase their momentum. In addition to overseeing the athletic training of a young man, the paidotribes taught him how to dance.

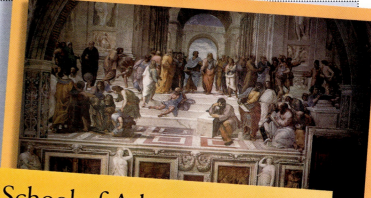

School of Athens

Artists and thinkers of the Italian **Renaissance** revered the rich legacy of Greek art and ideas. The artist Raphael (AD 1483-1520) painted an imaginary meeting of great men from different times in a **fresco** called *School of Athens (above).* Philosophers Plato and Aristotle stand in the center.

What's in a Name?

School

Skolle—the Greek word that gives us "school," meant simply "conversation" to the Greeks. They believed that learning could happen any-where, and encouraged young people to talk with their elders to become truly educated. Philosophers frequently met with their students in the gymnasium, where boys went to exercise. Citizens met to shop and discuss important issues of the day in the agora, which often resounded with heated debates. Simonides, a Greek poet, is famous for declaring that "the city is the teacher of man."

School Days

In a scene from a typical day at school on the drinking cup below, a boy reads from a scroll held by his grammatistes. Behind him sits his *paidagogos* —an older slave who accom-panied the boy to his lessons to make sure he paid attention.

On the left a music lesson is in progress. Boys completed their education between the ages of 15 and 18. After school they joined the army or learned a trade. Some boys continued to study with philosophers like Socrates, Plato, or Aristotle.

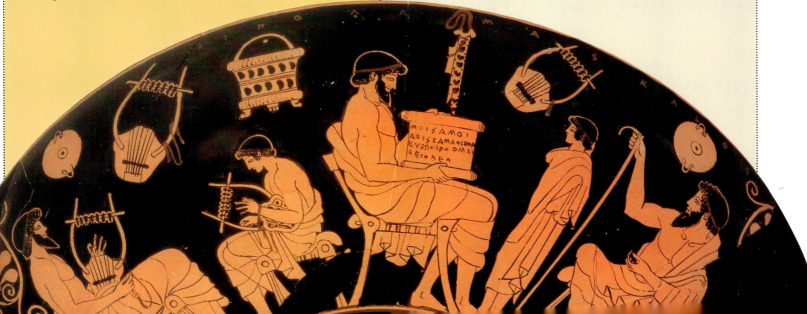

Actors & Athletes

The Olympics

G reeks loved to compete. They held contests for poetry, music, drama, and athletics to honor their gods, but their grandest spectacles were the Olympic Games. Every four years this five-day athletic festival was held in honor of Zeus. Athletes came from all over the Greek world to compete in foot-races, chariot races, wrestling matches, and other events. Greeks suspended wars so that spectators and athletes could travel safely to Olympia for the games. Victors were crowned with olive wreaths and treated as heroes for the rest of their lives. The games continued well into the **Christian era** until about AD 395, when new rulers abolished them as pagan rites. The tradition was revived in 1896 when the first modern Olympic Games were again held in Athens. Since then, the competition has brought the world together regularly to watch modern-day heroes compete for what is still an athlete's highest honor, an Olympic victory.

A Race of Their Own

Women were not allowed to compete in the Olympics. They could not even watch. Yet every four years they held their own festival, called the Heraia, in honor of Hera, Zeus's wife. The Heraia consisted of footraces *(above)* for three different age groups. Winners were crowned with an olive wreath.

At the Games

The first Olympics, held in 776 BC, consisted of a single 200-m (660-ft.) footrace. Later, other events, such as chariot racing and discus throwing *(left)*, were added. Many of the events—wrestling, running, and javelin throwing—grew out of military training exercises.

Athletes arrived at Olympia one month before the games began. Judges carefully observed them as they trained and selected the finest athletes to compete in the games. Athletes had no fancy gear; they competed in the nude. They rubbed their bodies with olive oil to make their skin shine before each event.

7 Wonders of the World

Zeus at Olympia

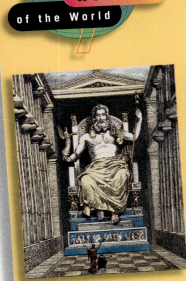

The colossal gold-and-ivory statue of Zeus that sat enthroned in the temple at Olympia was famous for its size and beauty. Though Zeus was seated, the statue stood more than 13 m (43 ft.) tall and was counted among the **Seven Wonders.** Ancient writers joked that if he should stand up, his head would come right through the temple's ceiling.

Let the Games Begin!

The stone starting blocks at Olympia *(left)* worked in much the same way as starting blocks do today. To make sure that all athletes started the race in the same place, ancient Olympians positioned their bare feet in the stone grooves, using them for traction when the race began.

Michael Johnson, whose golden sneakers are featured in the starting blocks below, won two gold medals and broke a world record in the 200-meter race in the 1996 Olympics in Atlanta. His sneakers recall the golden sandals of the fleet-footed god Hermes, to whom ancient athletes prayed for speed.

I Was There!

Epicitus, a philosopher and sports fan, recorded these thoughts about being at the Olympics in AD 100.

"Aren't you scorched there by the fierce heat? Aren't you crushed in the crowd? Isn't it difficult to freshen yourself up? Doesn't the rain soak you to the skin? Aren't you bothered by the noise, din, and other nuisances? But it seems to me that you are well able to bear and indeed gladly endure all this, when you think of what gripping spectacles you will see!"

Theater

All Greeks were encouraged to attend drama festivals, which could last for several days. In Athens, the state bought tickets for those who could not afford their own. Actors performed two types of plays at the festivals: Tragedies drew their themes from classical tales of heroes and their misfortunes. And comedies were rowdy, slapstick affairs that often poked fun at prominent citizens. Juries of citizens judged the plays and awarded the winning playwright a crown of ivy. Among the honored playwrights were Aeschylus, Sophocles, and Euripides, whose plays continue to be performed to this day.

All parts were played by men, who wore masks with wildly exaggerated expressions *(above)* to convey their characters' age, gender, and mood to the audience. Some theaters, like the well-preserved one at Epidaurus *(below),* could hold 14,000 spectators.

Ancient Persia

F ar to the east of Greece, in the country we know as Iran, lay the Persian **empire.** Between 600 and 400 BC Persian kings conquered neighboring lands, and the empire grew quickly. At its height it stretched from Egypt to India and reached as far north as the Caspian Sea. Babylonians, Assyrians, Phoenicians, Egyptians, and Indians fell under Persia's rule. To govern people with such different languages and cultures, Persian kings divided the empire into 20 provinces, each governed by an official called a **satrap.** They built roads and introduced a common currency, improving trade and communication between the far corners of their sprawling empire.

MACEDONIA
Athens
Halicarnassus
PERSIA
Susa
Perspolis
Indus R.
Arabian Sea

As Persia grew more powerful, it posed a threat to Greece. Twice in the fifth **century** BC Persia attempted to invade Greece. In 333 BC Alexander the Great struck back and by 330 BC had won the Persian empire for Greece.

Mausoleum of Halicarnassus

Wonders of the World

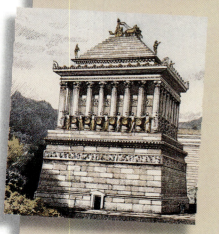

T his monumental tomb was built for Mausolus, the satrap of Halicarnassus on the coast of Turkey. It stood 42 m (120 ft.) tall and was covered on all four sides with elaborately carved statues. This "wonder" made such an impression on ancient travelers that "mausoleum" became a general term for any large tomb.

Persian Motels

T ravelers along Persia's Royal Road *(below)* never had to worry about finding a place to spend the night. More than 100 inns lined the highway between Susa and Ephesus. They were spaced about 25 km (15 mi.), or one day's journey, apart. Royal messengers could change horses there and ride on to deliver their news.

Golden Treasures

P ersian kings amassed a staggering treasury of gold through tribute and conquest. The golden armband *(right)* and miniature gold chariot *(below)* from the time of Darius III were found near the Amu Darya River in Persia in the 19th century.

Golden Armband

Chariot

Darius's treasury held a hoard of 4,500 tons of gold and silver. When Alexander sacked the palace, he exclaimed, "So this is what it means to be a king!"

Gifts of Tribute

Every year, dignitaries from Persia's provinces ascended the Grand Staircase at Persepolis *(above, right)* to present tribute to King Darius III *(far right)*. Their offerings depended on the riches of their particular region; some brought stallions and camels, whereas others came with fine perfumes and textiles. Many, like the Indian at right, brought baskets laden with gold. Darius came to consider himself a god-king. He commanded that visitors before his throne cover their mouth and bend deeply at the waist to show their reverence for him.

The Immortals

Members of Persia's elite royal guard were called the Ten Thousand Immortals. When one fell in battle, a new soldier immediately stepped in to take his place. The "immortal" above carries an ivory bow and a quiver of arrows on his back.

Alexander the Great

At age 20, Alexander ruled Greece. At 24 he was crowned **pharaoh** of Egypt. At 26, after conquering the vast Persian **empire,** Alexander the Great ruled the largest empire the world had ever known.

How did one man accomplish so much? In 336 BC, he inherited Greece from his father, King Philip of Macedonia. Philip was a general who made sure that Alexander had the finest military training as a boy. Alexander took up his father's campaign to conquer the Persian empire. With 35,000 soldiers he marched east and south, winning battle after battle and gaining riches for Greece. He founded many cities named Alexandria. The most famous one, in Egypt, became a center for trade and learning.

When Alexander reached India, his weary troops urged him to turn back. Shortly thereafter, in 323 BC, Alexander died of a fever in Babylon at age 33. His generals divided his empire among themselves. Greece prospered until about 190 BC, when rivalries erupted among the provinces. The final blow came in 146 BC with the Roman conquest of Greece.

Alexander

Alexander was known as much for his love of learning as for his courage. During his march of conquest he wanted to spread Greek art and culture to his new empire and at the same time learn everything about these regions. Greek scholars accompanied the army to record information about the geography, plants, animals, and religions. Alexander's library, with more than 10,000 scrolls, traveled with him. It is said that he slept with a copy of Homer's *Iliad* under his pillow.

Alexandria

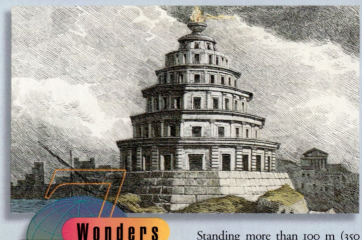

7 Wonders of the World

Pharos Lighthouse

Standing more than 100 m (350 ft.) tall, the massive Pharos, or lighthouse, of Alexandria was the most spectacular of its kind in the ancient world. Bronze mirrors at the top reflected light from fire and light from the sun as far as 48 km (30 mi.) out to sea to guide boats into port.

Alexander's Empire

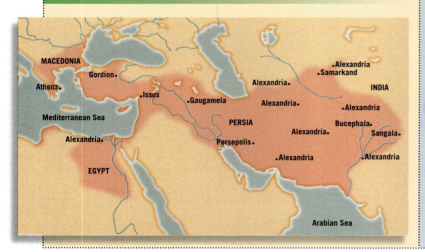

MACEDONIA
Athens
Gordion
Issus
Mediterranean Sea
Alexandria
EGYPT
Gaugamela
Alexandria
PERSIA
Persepolis
Alexandria
Alexandria
Samarkand
INDIA
Alexandria
Bucephala
Alexandria
Sangala
Alexandria
Arabian Sea

Battle of Issus

In 333 BC at the Battle of Issus in Persia, Darius III *(in chariot, right)* turns to flee from Alexander's relentless advance, as retold in this **mosaic.** The battle marked the beginning of the end for the Persian empire. Darius did not surrender, but he abandoned his war tents, and even his family, as he fled into the mountains.

Check This Out!

Ptolemy I, one of Alexander's generals and the new pharaoh of Egypt, wanted to make Alexandria a center of learning. In the early third **century** BC, he built a library *(below)* and collected close to 500,000 scrolls on subjects such as astronomy, physics, medicine, mathematics, poetry, and philosophy on its many-tiered shelves. The library represented the largest collection of knowledge the world had ever known.

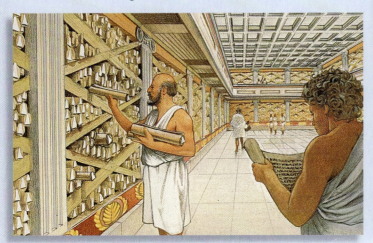

Eureka!

Archimedes' screw

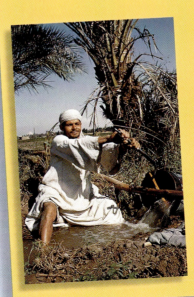

Archimedes was one of the most gifted scholars to study at Alexandria. He invented the water screw *(diagram)*, which allowed farmers to raise water from a low level to a higher one to irrigate their fields. Some farmers in Egypt *(left)* continue to use this method. Archimedes is also famous for discovering how to calculate the volume of an object by placing it in a tank of water. The amount of water the object displaces—by making the water rise—is equal to the object's volume. He discovered this principle when he sat in his bath and saw the water rise. He jumped up and shouted, "Eureka!" which means "I found it!"

Rome Republic to Empire

No one is sure of the beginnings of Rome, but by the 10th **century** BC, people were already farming the land along the banks of the Tiber River in what is now central Italy. There Rome grew from a simple village to a mighty **empire**. At first, Rome was ruled by Etruscan kings from the north. When the last one was overthrown in 509 BC, Roman landowners formed a council of leaders, the Senate. They called their country the **republic**—from the words in their **Latin** language meaning "affairs of the people."

Over the next 400 years Rome added the rest of Italy to the republic and took over much of Europe, western Asia, and North Africa. When Julius Caesar came to power in 47 BC, the city of Rome had more than 150,000 inhabitants. Caesar's heirs became absolute **monarchs**, reigning over an expanding empire. In AD 286, Emperor Diocletian split the empire into east and west, with a ruler for each. The eastern empire, with its capital at Constantinople, lasted until AD 1453.

Would You Believe?

Children of the Wolf

This ancient statue illustrates the Roman legend of twins Romulus and Remus, which says that these royal descendants of a Trojan War hero were left to die on the banks of the Tiber River. Rescued from starvation by a wolf, they were raised by a shepherd and established a city where they had been found. The brothers argued over who should name and rule the city, and Romulus killed Remus to become king.

900-500 BC	500-31 BC	31 BC-AD 68
Latin Tribes	**Republic**	**Early Empire**

Etruscans

Etruscan people from central Italy, such as those shown as statues below, influenced Latin culture with a religion based on Greek deities, as well as with their alphabet and their realistic art forms.

Julius Caesar

An ambitious general, Caesar became sole ruler in Rome in 47 BC, destroying the two-consul leadership system of the republic.

Augustus and Nero

Augustus Caesar succeeded his uncle Julius Caesar, becoming emperor in 31 BC. His 40-year reign is called Rome's golden age. Under his rule, Jesus was born in Bethlehem. Years later the emperor Nero, who ruled from AD 54 to 68, was known for his interest in the arts as well as for his cruelty and persecution of Christians.

Food for All

Early reform leaders Tiberius and Gaius Gracchus insisted that the Roman republic should take good care of its citizens. They said that the republic should give public lands to farmers and sell grain to poor citizens at special low prices. After the republic became an empire, grain was given for free to the needy.

AD 69-235
High Empire

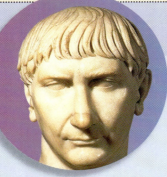

Trajan and Hadrian

Spanish-born Trajan was an army general when the Senate made him emperor in AD 98. Under his able leadership the empire reached its greatest extent. He conquered Dacia (now Romania) and built a new forum and **aqueducts** to improve water supplies. Hadrian, Trajan's successor in AD 117, traveled all over the empire, making sure the far-off frontiers were defended. His army built Hadrian's Wall, a fortification along the Scottish border.

AD 476
Fall of Western Empire

Constantine

Constantine changed the character of the empire by granting religious tolerance to Christians in AD 311. Undoing Diocletian's legacy, he reunited the split empire in AD 324 but established an eastern capital in the old city of Byzantium and renamed it Constantinople. When Rome fell to the Vandals in AD 476, destroying the empire in the west, emperors continued to rule the east under Roman principles for another thousand years.

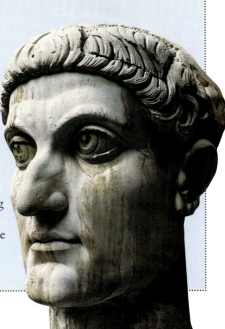

Forum Center of Power

The Roman Forum was the center of government, religion, commerce, and public life. Originally an open market square, the Forum was filled by **generations** of builders with temples to the city gods; a platform where senators made speeches to the crowds; the Curia, where the Senate met; and arches celebrating military victories. The bronze **tablets** that recorded the laws of Rome were kept in a temple in the Forum along with the national treasury. Every important event in the long history of the **republic** and the **empire** either took place in the Forum or was discussed there.

Prominent citizens, senators, and members of patrician families visited the Forum daily. There they would meet their friends, get the news of the day, shop, or perform their duties in the governing of Rome.

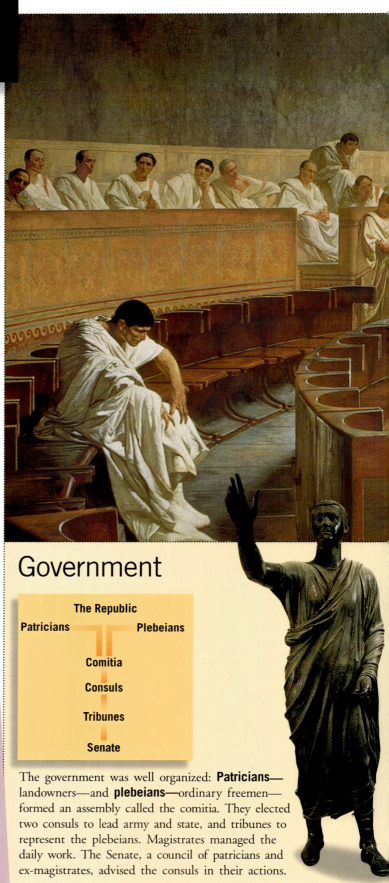

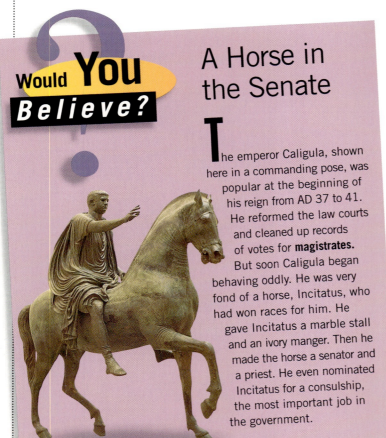

Would You Believe?

A Horse in the Senate

The emperor Caligula, shown here in a commanding pose, was popular at the beginning of his reign from AD 37 to 41. He reformed the law courts and cleaned up records of votes for **magistrates.** But soon Caligula began behaving oddly. He was very fond of a horse, Incitatus, who had won races for him. He gave Incitatus a marble stall and an ivory manger. Then he made the horse a senator and a priest. He even nominated Incitatus for a consulship, the most important job in the government.

Government

The Republic		
Patricians		Plebeians
	Comitia	
	Consuls	
	Tribunes	
	Senate	

The government was well organized: **Patricians**—landowners—and **plebeians**—ordinary freemen—formed an assembly called the comitia. They elected two consuls to lead army and state, and tribunes to represent the plebeians. Magistrates managed the daily work. The Senate, a council of patricians and ex-magistrates, advised the consuls in their actions.

The Senate

The Roman Senate was a powerful ruling force in the days of the republic. Its leaders influenced the decisions of consuls, controlled the republic's money, and voted to accept or reject any acts of the comitia. During the empire, the Senate voted to confirm emperors and their heirs. More than a thousand years later, the framers of the Constitution of the United States established a Senate modeled on Rome's to make laws and to confirm state policy. The U.S. Senate meets in a chamber *(above)* that looks very much like the Roman one.

Then & NOW!

The Forum

The picture at left re-creates the ancient Roman Forum as it would have looked about AD 200. The photo below shows the same place today, its ruins surrounded by newer buildings. You can see the marble Arch of Septimus Severus at the right in both pictures. The speakers' platform dominates the center of both pictures. Today the Forum is famous for its large population of homeless cats. Actress Whoopi Goldberg *(right)* starred in *A Funny Thing Happened on the Way to the Forum,* a musical based on plays by the Roman author Titus Maccius Plautus (254-184 BC).

Patrician Ways

Patrician families were the aristocracy of Rome. They consisted of landowning nobles whose **ancestors** had been powerful since the days of the Etruscan kings. **Patricians** held special privileges. At first they were the only ones allowed to become **magistrates** and senators. Later, a common person, or **plebeian,** could be elected consul, at which time he automatically became a noble. Wealthy Romans, patrician or not, usually owned large tracts of land where they kept country houses, or villas. They also lived part of the year in Rome. Their large townhouses included courtyard gardens and outbuildings. Every household had at least a few slaves to do the chores; wealthy families had hundreds.

Some slaveholders were cruel masters. Others saw to it that a faithful servant would be freed after the owner's death. A few slaves managed to carry out their own business on the side and could eventually buy their freedom. Freed slaves still did not have the same status as Roman citizens, but the next **generation**—their children—did. Once a slave became a freedman he could own slaves as well.

Education

Like the child in this wall painting, the youngest Romans were taught by their mothers. Rich families sent both girls and boys to private school at about seven years old. Some families hired tutors, who were often educated Greek slaves, to teach children at home. Teachers were strict and often punished students severely. Children studied reading, writing, and arithmetic. They wrote by pressing sharpened sticks into wax-coated boards, then smoothed out the wax and used the board again. Some boys went on to further schooling at age 12 and learned Greek, history, geometry, and astronomy and how to make good speeches.

Marriage

Among patricians marriage was a business arrangement. In the wedding scene at left, the groom holds a marriage contract as well as his bride's hand. The contract was an important document that set out all the responsibilities and conditions of the marriage. As a new head of household, the groom would have legal control over the family lands, possessions, any children of the marriage, and, often, his new wife. Family responsibilities included many other relatives, too: Cousins, uncles, aunts, and grandparents became tied together in a complicated tangle of rights and duties.

A Townhouse

Elegant Roman townhouses had no windows onto the street. They were built around courtyards for privacy and safety. The public part of the house below contained a kitchen, a receiving room called an atrium that was open to the sky, and storage and servants' rooms. Surrounding the garden were bedrooms and a living room.

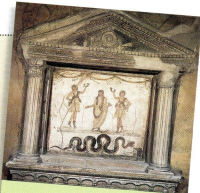

Household Gods

Shrines like the one above were devoted to the household gods. Spirits of house and land were called lares, guardians of food and wealth were penates, and an ancestral spirit was called the genius of the family. Once a day Romans presented incense, wine, fire, and prayers to their special gods.

Wear a Roman Toga

Try it!

Romans wore a toga of wool or linen over their short tunics. To make your own toga, use a piece of cloth at least 1.8 m (6 ft.) long and about 1 m (3 ft.) wide. Hang one end over your left shoulder down to your ankle in front. Drape the other end around your back, under your right arm, and over your left shoulder so the rest hangs down behind. Pin your toga at the shoulder.

Protective Bulla

Both girls and boys wore charms called bullae around their necks. These were meant to protect them from evil spirits. Boys like the one at right wore them until they were 14, then dedicated them to the guardian spirits of the family. A girl wore her bulla until she married.

Roman Numerals

Numbers larger than 10 are made by adding on the largest numbers possible. For instance, 16 is written as XVI (10 plus 6). A small number placed to the left of a larger one is subtracted from it. So CM means 1,000 minus 100, or 900.

1 = I	8 = VIII
2 = II	9 = IX
3 = III	10 = X
4 = IV	50 = L
5 = V	100 = C
6 = VI	500 = D
7 = VII	1,000 = M
MCMXCVIII = 1998	

Communal Life in the City

The citizens of Rome thought their city was the most exciting place in the world. You could see people and goods from all the provinces of the **empire.** Soldiers, parades, and religious processions filled the streets. Senators argued and inspired the crowds in the Forum. The Circus Maximus hosted races, the Colosseum held games and shows, and even the local market might offer the spectacle of rival fish sellers fighting for a customer.

Romans spent a lot of time meeting friends and conducting business outdoors. So many people thronged the streets that cart traffic was banned during the day. The writer Juvenal described the scene: "You get dug in the ribs by someone's elbow. Then someone hits you with a long pole, another with a beam from a building or a wine-barrel. The streets are filthy—our legs are plastered with mud, and someone tramples our feet."

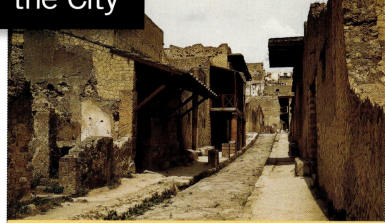

Apartment Living

Plebeians lived in apartments that lined narrow streets. These buildings were up to six stories high. Families shared three or four rooms on one floor and used public latrines on the street (*above, right).* Landlords were often greedy, slow to make repairs, and hated by their tenants.

Banquets

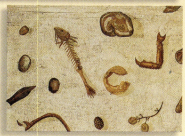

The guests in the wall painting at left are attending a special feast. Such a meal was served by slaves who set out the food on low tables. The diners stretched out at their ease on couches, eating with their fingers. The drink of choice was wine, sometimes sweetened with honey.

Guests would simply throw any bones or leftovers on the floor; dogs would do the cleanup. The **mosaic** at left, once the floor of a formal dining room, shows just what it would have looked like after a good Roman dinner party.

Strange But TRUE! A Roman Menu

A famous Roman cookbook suggested the food below as a suitable meal for a banquet. Romans liked to sample exotic dishes—such as flamingo and ostrich—from far provinces of the empire.

Appetizers
Jellyfish and eggs
Sow's udders stuffed with sea urchins
Patina of brains cooked with milk and eggs
Boiled tree fungi with peppered fish-fat sauce

Main Course
Boiled ostrich with sweet sauce
Turtledove boiled in its feathers
Roast parrot
Flamingo boiled with dates

Dessert
Stoned dates stuffed with nuts and pine kernels, fried in honey
Hot African sweet-wine cakes with honey

SPLASH !

Roman author Lucius Seneca (5 BC-AD 65) complained: *"I live over the public baths—you know what that means. Ugh! It's sickening. First there are the 'strongmen' doing their exercises and swinging heavy lead weights about with grunts and groans. . . . Then there is the noise of a brawler or thief being arrested and the man who always likes the sound of his own voice in the bath. And what about the ones who leap into the pool making a huge splash as they hit the water!"*

At the Baths

Romans built this pool complex in Bath, England, at a natural spring in the first **century** AD. Like other Roman baths, it contained pools with lukewarm, hot, and cold water. Since few houses had private bathrooms, people of all classes visited public baths. First they would dip into the pools, then cover their bodies with oil. A servant would scrape off the oil with a bone or metal strip. Professional trainers, sometimes ex-**gladiators,** helped people exercise in special gyms, as the mosaic lady at left is doing. Or one could simply read, gossip, and relax.

Bread & Circus

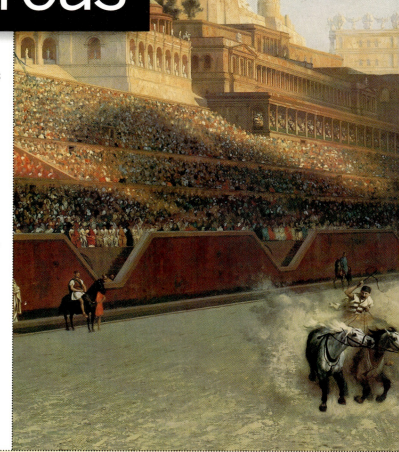

Cheered by 250,000 screaming fans, charioteers tore around the sharp turns at the Circus Maximus in pursuit of lavish prizes and perhaps a bonus from the emperor. Chariot teams had four horses. Teams were known by their colors—blue, green, red, and white—and each of these was associated with a political faction. People bet on the races, and riots and fights were common.

The Etruscan kings established the Circus Maximus, and throughout Rome's history the government used public games and shows to keep the people amused. The writer Juvenal said that Romans were easily satisfied with no more than bread and circuses. Emperors often proclaimed public holidays with parades, games, and free feasts to celebrate a military triumph or mark their own birthdays. Traditional celebrations included a harvest festival and days set aside to honor the god Jupiter.

The Top Twelve

Romans reserved their deepest religious feelings for their household gods. Country people worshiped the ancient nature gods of their own areas: water and plant spirits, the sun, and the corn goddess. But the official state religion was based on gods adopted from the Greeks. Several of the Caesars were also worshiped as gods after they died, making religious practice a patriotic duty. The chart at right shows the most important gods.

Let's Compare

Greek	Roman	
Zeus	Jupiter	King of the gods
Hera	Juno	Jupiter's wife, guardian of wives
Hestia	Vesta	Protector of hearth and home
Ares	Mars	God of war and battles
Apollo	Apollo	God of music, healing, the sun
Athena	Minerva	Goddess of wisdom and industry
Poseidon	Neptune	God of the sea
Hermes	Mercury	God of messengers and trade
Aphrodite	Venus	Goddess of love and beauty
Artemis	Diana	Goddess of the hunt and animals
Demeter	Ceres	Goddess of grain and the harvest
Hephaistos	Vulcan	God of fire and blacksmithing

Circus Maximus

Originally just a level field where citizens could watch the races, the Circus Maximus was later improved with seats on three sides and a covered pavilion. The course measured about 180 m (600 ft.) across and 600 m (2,000 ft.) long. Horses raced seven times around the track before crossing the finish line.

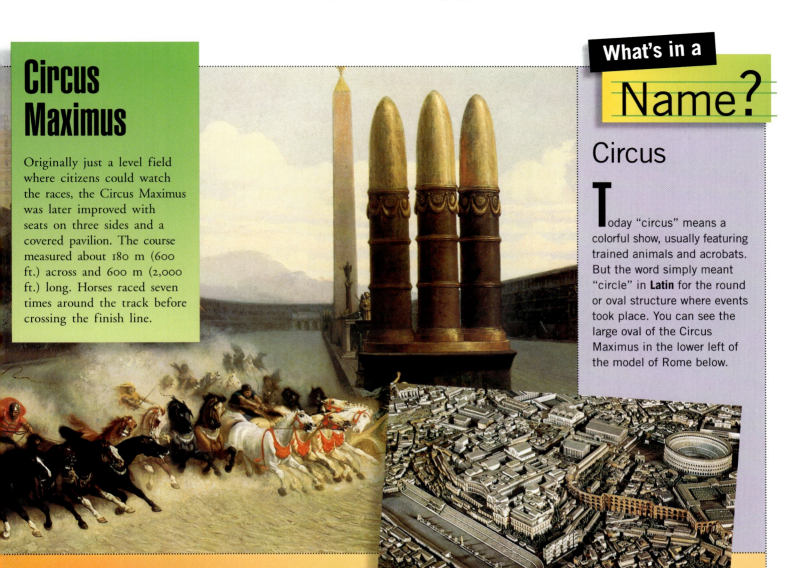

Circus

Today "circus" means a colorful show, usually featuring trained animals and acrobats. But the word simply meant "circle" in **Latin** for the round or oval structure where events took place. You can see the large oval of the Circus Maximus in the lower left of the model of Rome below.

Holidays and Festivals

Religious holidays featured parades, animal **sacrifices,** and games held in honor of the gods at the Colosseum *(left and in model above)*. This was the arena for professional fighters—**gladiators** *(below, right)*—in their bloody combats with each other or with wild beasts. The Colosseum could also be flooded to stage mock sea battles.

The Roman year began in March, when everyone celebrated days dedicated to Mars and the military. Autumn brought harvest feasts, whereas December was marked by a long festival called Saturnalia. During Saturnalia people wore costumes, gave each other gifts, and held banquets.

Working for a Living

The busy city of Rome was the marketplace of the Mediterranean world in the days of the **empire.** Almost anything you could want—and many things never before seen—could be found and bought there. Merchants dealt in foreign treasures, including artwork, silks, and fancy furniture, but many goods also came from local **artisans;** there were 150 trade associations for craftsmen.

Because Romans ate a lot of bread, bakeries and cookshops flourished throughout the city. Meats, fish, and vegetables were sold in small shops or in the marketplace by farmers who came in from the country for the day. The constant construction of public and private buildings meant gangs of carpenters, plasterers, masons, and wall painters swarmed everywhere. Workshops, employing three or four workers, made glass or metal objects. Private fire brigades—men with buckets directed by a foreman—bargained for their fees with owners of burning buildings before throwing water on the blaze. Soldiers came to Rome on leave from militia duty in the faraway provinces.

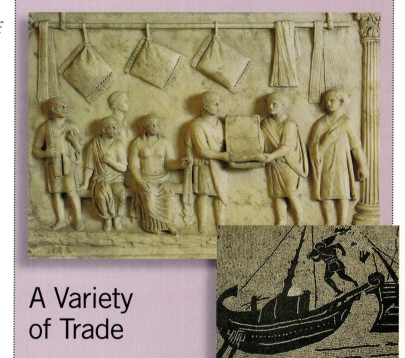

A Variety of Trade

Rome was filled with tradespeople. Merchants worked from specialized shops, such as the fabric store above, selling food and other goods shipped up the Tiber from ports on the coast. **Mosaics** *(above)* set in the street outside each shop advertised the trades in the port city.

Wild Beasts for Sale

Animals like the elephant and wild ox (note the safety bar on its horns) being loaded aboard a ship on the coast of North Africa were destined for the circus in Rome. The African provinces also supplied Rome with wheat, gold, and spices.

Farming

Farms near Rome produced the wheat, olives, fruit, and cattle that sustained the city. Teams of oxen provided the power to plow the fields, as shown in the mosaic below; large landowners rented land to tenants and kept slaves to work their fields.

Making Wine

Everywhere the Romans went, they planted grapevines to make their favorite drink: wine. At the autumn harvest, pickers dumped baskets of ripe grapes into shallow vats, where treaders crushed them under their bare feet. It was slippery work—the two men shown here must hold onto each other and their support poles so they won't fall. Winemakers allowed the resulting juice to ferment, then stored it in pottery jugs. Romans liked their wine watered and warm.

The Professions

Many Romans used the services of teachers, doctors, and lawyers, though these professions were not much respected. Doctors and teachers often were Greek ex-slaves. Teachers advertised for students—and sometimes had trouble collecting their fees from the parents. The army maintained its own doctors, like this one carefully removing an arrowhead from a wounded leg.

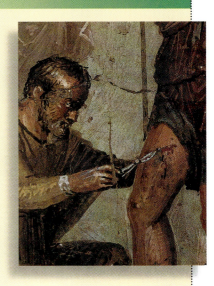

Buried by the Volcano

August 24, AD 79. As the citizens of Pompeii— a resort town 130 miles south of Rome—awoke, they noticed a column of smoke and ash rising from the nearby volcano Vesuvius. By afternoon, ash and pieces of pumice, a light rock, were falling. Sounds of explosions came from the volcano. By 5:00 p.m., several feet of ash and pumice had fallen, and roofs began to collapse. Frightened people ran outdoors and were outside at midnight when hot clouds of gas and rock poured down and covered the town.

Throughout the night, ash, poisonous gas, and rock bombarded Pompeii and the nearby town of Herculaneum. Some people escaped to the seashore, but most were felled by pieces of rock or choked by ash and gas. Seven feet of debris covered Pompeii, hiding its theater, homes, marketplace, and the bodies of its people.

And so it remained for nearly 1,700 years. **Archaeologists** began digging into the buried cities in the 19th century, uncovering a Roman **civilization** preserved in ash, as if in a time capsule.

Then & NOW!

A Villa in Pompeii

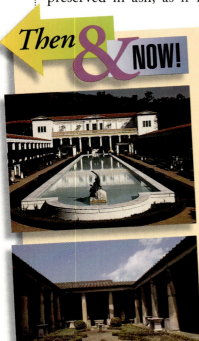

In AD 79 the Villa of the Papyri near Herculaneum must have looked much like this reconstruction *(above, left)* at the J. Paul Getty Museum in California. The original, with its large pool where fish for the kitchen could be raised, was discovered under 20 m (65 ft.) of rock. A similar villa from Herculaneum is shown at left as it was **excavated** in recent times.

Living in Luxury

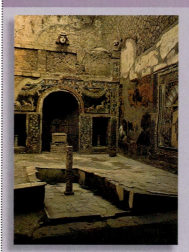

Dining Room

The wine merchant who owned this townhouse in Pompeii more than 1,900 years ago hosted banquets in the courtyard at left. Diners could admire the richly colored wall paintings and be soothed by the tinkle of the central fountain as they ate. A guest wrote on the wall of one such home: "How inviting is your house, O Albucius!"

The Ruins of Pompeii

The threatening mass of Vesuvius looms behind the ruins of Pompeii's Forum. The buildings that stood here, once brightly painted in red, yellow, and green, included a Temple of Jupiter, city offices, the Basilica—or law court—and a hall serving the clothmakers' guild. The Forum had already been damaged by an earthquake in AD 62; some structures were being rebuilt at the time the volcano erupted.

I Was There!

Vittorio Di Girolamo, assistant supervisor at Herculaneum, carefully brushes the dust and ashes from the bones of a Roman soldier. The way the skeleton is lying in the volcanic ash suggests that the soldier was running toward the beach when he died in the volcanic eruption. His sword lies by his right side, and the buckle of a tool kit can be seen across his back. Physical anthropologists who examined many of these bones can piece together much about who these people were and how they lived.

Among the many buried **artifacts** in Pompeii, archaeologists uncovered a hoard of silver dishes like this double-handled drinking cup. The finely hammered and sculpted silver object was a luxury item. Silver cups, plates, and serving bowls came in sets of as many as 100 pieces. The valuable serving pieces were passed on to the children, as is done with the family silver today.

Drinking Cup

Building the Empire

Romans were famous for their construction skills. Roman buildings and roads still exist—and are still used—all across Europe, the Near East, and North Africa today.

Wherever the Romans went, they built in the same recognizable style: theaters in the round, straight roads paved with fitted stone, temples and public offices with columns across the front. Engineers used the rounded arch to frame doors, create wide-span bridges, and form the huge monuments called triumphal arches placed over roads to mark military victories. Builders preferred to work with stone, so masons grew skillful at fitting blocks together without mortar. The invention of concrete, a mixture of lime mortar and sand that dried to stonelike hardness, allowed Romans to erect tall structures.

Roman Roads

The Appian Way *(above)*, begun near Rome in 312 BC, was a prime example of the roads Romans built across the **empire.** As one writer said: "Its breadth is such that two wagons going in opposite directions can easily pass one another . . . the stones are so finely cut, leveled and fitted together without mortar that the unbroken surface appears to be not the work of man, but a wondrous **phenomenon** of nature."

The crossing blocks *(inset)* in Pompeii let pedestrians cross from sidewalk to sidewalk without getting muddy.

Christian Catacombs

Romans feared the early Christians. They rejected the Roman gods; and the province of Judea, where Jesus preached, had a history of violent revolt. Emperor Nero (AD 54-68) made persecution of Christians a public policy. He blamed them for plagues and for a disastrous fire and sent many to be killed by wild beasts in the Colosseum.

Christians preferred to bury their dead, rather than cremate them as was the Roman custom. Because they were barred from central cemeteries, they used tunnels cut through rock outside the city instead. In these **catacombs,** bodies were laid to rest on ledges along the sides of the tunnels. Christians gathered there, both to honor their dead martyrs and to stay hidden from the authorities.

Would You Believe?

A Crane with Man Power

Clever construction machines like the crane at right helped Romans put up large buildings even in remote places. At its top was a platform where masons perched. Men walking a treadmill at the crane's base raised the platform with ropes and pulleys.

The Pantheon

Roman architects built the Pantheon from concrete between AD 118 and AD 128 as a temple to honor all the gods. The huge dome, which is still standing, was poured in layers around a wooden mold. It measures 33 m (142 ft.) across at floor level and 33 m (142 ft.) high inside. No larger dome was built for 400 years.

Raising an Arch

The Romans found a new way to construct arches by setting stones or bricks on a wooden frame, working from both sides toward the middle. When they laid the central keystone, they took away the wood. Bricks pressing outward and down from the keystone held the arch together and made it strong.

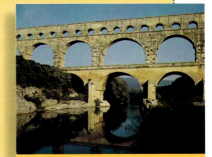

Aqueducts

Built by Roman soldiers on duty in the provinces, the Pont du Gard, an **aqueduct** in southern France, once channeled water to a city 48 km (30 mi.) away. Most Roman watercourses ran underground to keep the water clean. Roman towns were known for good public water supplies and sewers to carry away waste.

The Roman Legions

Warfare was an amateur business in the early days of the republic. Soldiers were chosen from a yearly assembly of landowners. Each unpaid recruit brought his own weapons and armor and would defend only his own city. By imperial times the army had changed. Legions were permanent and professional. Their troops were paid, equipped with armor and weapons, and trained to fight against enemies who lived far from Rome. Auxiliaries, native troops from the frontiers, could become Roman citizens after serving. With these, Rome had about 300,000 soldiers. A new recruit learned to march, swim, and fight using packs and weapons twice the weight of the real ones, to build up his strength. He practiced with swords and the pilum, a heavy spear with a metal head. Soldiers like the one at left wore helmets, armor made of metal plates attached to a leather harness, boots or sandals, and cloaks in winter. Military camps included barracks, workshops, a market, bathhouse, and theater. Soldiers built camps in a square behind ramparts or walls. Soldiers also built roads across the empire, making sure Rome could quickly send forces to defend any of the far-flung provinces. Legionnaires enlisted for 25 years. Veterans chose a piece of land or a cash payment as their retirement bonus.

How Many?

The Army

A Roman legion numbered 5,000 men divided into nine cohorts of about 500 each, plus an elite cohort of 800 men. Cohorts were made up of five or more centuries—originally 100 soldiers, later reduced to 80. The standing army had 28 legions.

Siege!

The Roman army brought state-of-the-art skills and equipment to attacks. Here they have built timber ramps so that tall siege towers, filled with soldiers, can roll up to the top of the wall. Holding shields that cover them in the formation called a *testudo,* or "tortoise," more troops advance along the ramp. The artillery uses ballistas *(bottom right)* to hurl rocks at the walls, while onagers *(bottom)* fling flaming logs.

Imagine That!

Elephant Attacks!

Elephants attacked Rome not once but twice in the third **century** BC. King Pyrrhus of Greece used 20 of the beasts, trained to charge like live tanks. Though he won that battle, he lost the war. Soon thereafter Hannibal, war leader of Carthage, a Phoenician port in North Africa, drove 37 elephants across the Alps to attack Rome from the north. He managed to conquer most of Italy but never took Rome.

A Famous Defeat

The German warrior Hermann, shown at left in mounted triumph, won a devastating victory over Rome in AD 9, when his German tribesmen defeated three Roman legions and auxiliaries led by military governor Quinctilius Varus in the swamps of Germany's Teutoburg Forest. The Germans even captured the legions' precious eagle standards, like the one at right, which deeply humiliated the Romans.

The Glory That Was Rome

When Emperor Trajan died in AD 117, the Roman **empire** stretched across 5 million sq. km (2 million sq. mi.) and included 43 foreign provinces. The outlines of this area can be seen on the map at right. Provinces paid taxes to Rome and submitted to Roman rule, receiving free schooling, libraries, theaters, circuses, grain for the poor, and trade advantages. Roman laws were the same throughout the empire, and provinces were protected from enemy invasion by the force of the legions.

But the benefits of Roman **civilization** could not hold together such a spread-out state forever. Tribes from outside the empire attacked the borders again and again, while army rebellions swept favored generals into and out of power.

When Diocletian divided the empire in AD 286, quarrels broke out between the two halves. Northern settlers moved into Spain and Italy; Rome itself was captured and sacked twice. In AD 476, an army of Germanic tribesmen drove the emperor from his throne and the long rule of Rome in the west was ended.

Hadrian's Wall

Emperor Hadrian ordered this 118-km (73-mi.)-long wall to be built along the border between the Roman province of Britain and the wild tribes of Scotland. Guard posts were placed every mile; several large camps supported the permanent army stationed there.

Theaters

Every provincial town of any size in the empire had an open-air theater like this one, still in use at Orange, France. Built by the army, the theaters helped entertain the troops during peacetime.

Volubilis

The **mosaic** floors of this villa in Volubilis (in modern Morocco) make a stark contrast with the desert beyond. Volubilis was the farthest western outpost of the Roman Empire in North Africa. Roman engineers built a temple, forum, and law courts there, as well as an **aqueduct** to provide the city with fresh water. North Africa in turn sent Rome grain, colored marble, and exotic animals.

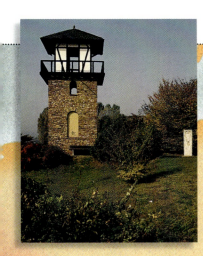

Frontier Forts

This stone-and-timber watch-tower, restored to its original appearance, stands along the Roman border on the Rhine River in Germany. It guards a wall still called the Limes, from the **Latin** word for border, or limit. The Limes was the northernmost edge of the empire in Germany; beyond it lived the barbarian enemies of Rome. The next watchtower was less than a half mile away.

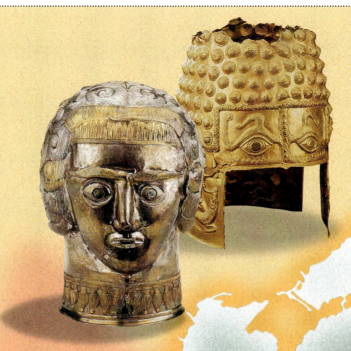

Dacian Gold

The frowning gold-and-silver head and gold helmet above were made in Dacia, north of the Balkans. Dacians harried Roman borders on the Danube until Trajan subdued them in a bloody war from AD 101 to 106. The area became a province (modern Romania) that Rome exploited for its silver, gold, and iron. The Romanian language is based on Latin, and boys there are still named Traian after Trajan.

Library at Ephesus

The Library at Ephesus (in modern Turkey) was the second-largest library in ancient times. The library, with its stately marble columns, was built by Trajan when this city stood at one end of the trade route into Asia. The Romans kept a channel open from the city's old Greek center to its port on the Aegean Sea. Here also stood the Temple of Artemis *(page 83)*.

Timeline Chronology of Events

	3500-2000 BC	2000-1500 BC	1500-1000 BC
Sumer/ Middle East 	**c. 3500** City of Ur founded **c. 3100** Sumerians develop first known system of writing **c.2300** Sargon conquers Sumerians, unites all of Mesopotamia	**c. 2000** Phoenicians begin building city-states **c. 1800** In Mesopotamia, Code of Hammurabi is written **c. 1500** Cuneiform script appears in Mesopotamia	**c. 1020** Hebrews found kingdom of Israel **c. 1200** Phoenicians trade all around the Mediterranean
Egypt and Nubia	**c. 3100** Unification of Upper and Lower Egypt under King Narmer **c. 3000** Beginning of Nubian civilization **c. 2700-2200** Old Kingdom **2540** Construction of Great Pyramid at Giza begins	**c. 2000** Mentuhotep reunites Egypt after a period of war **c. 2000-1660** Middle Kingdom	**1560-1070** New Kingdom **c. 1350** King Tut buried in the Valley of the Kings **1304-1237** Rule of Ramses the Great 
China and India	**c. 3000** Farming begins in Yellow River Valley, China **c. 2700** Chinese start casting bronze and spinning silk **c. 2200** Legendary Xia dynasty begins in China **c. 2500-1900** Indus Valley civilization	**c. 1766-1122** Shang dynasty, China **c. 1500** Nomads settle Ganges Valley in India; spread of Hinduism	**c. 1100-256** Zhou dynasty in China develops a bureaucracy with ranked nobility
Greece and Rome 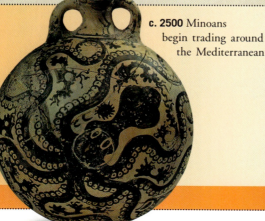	**c. 2500** Minoans begin trading around the Mediterranean	**c. 2000-1400** Minoan civilization **c. 1600-1100** Mycenaean civilization	**c. 1200** Historical date of Trojan War

1000-500 BC

1000 David makes Jerusalem his capital

961-922 Reign of King Solomon

c. 550 Cyrus the Great of Persia invades Mesopotamia

c. 770 Kushite rulers from Nubia conquer Egypt

c. 670 King Taharqa rules as pharaoh of Egypt and Nubia

c. 560-483 Life of the Buddha

551-479 Life of Confucius

c. 900 State of Sparta founded

c. 900-500 Etruscan civilization flourishes in Italy

c. 800-700 *Iliad* and *Odyssey* recorded by Homer

776 First Olympic Games, Greece

753 City of Rome founded on Tiber River in Italy

509 Roman Republic established

500-1 BC

c. 500 Darius I improves government and communications in Persia

330 Darius III of Persia defeated by Alexander the Great; Persian empire ends

323 Ptolemy I becomes pharaoh, builds Library of Alexandria

30 Egypt becomes a Roman province

c. 279 Asoka establishes first Indian empire

221 Unification of China by first Qin emperor

AD 202-220 Han dynasty, China

c. 200 Building of Great Wall of China begun

c. 100 Trade on Silk Road

448 Construction of Parthenon in Athens

333 Alexander the Great begins 10-year campaign in Asia

146 Romans conquer Greece

31 Roman Empire begins under Augustus

AD 1-500

1 Christian era begins

135 Romans destroy Jerusalem, ban Jews from entering

c. 500 End of Kushite kingdom in Meroë

c. 50 Buddhism reaches China

c. 100 Papermaking invented in China

320 India begins golden age under the Gupta dynasty

79 Eruption of Vesuvius buries Pompeii, Herculaneum

116 Roman Empire reaches greatest extent under Trajan

330 Constantinople becomes capital of eastern Roman Empire, Rome remains capital in west

476 Western half of Roman Empire collapses

Picture Credits

The sources for the illustrations are listed below. Credits from left to right are separated by semicolons, from top to bottom by dashes.

Cover: book spine, Bildarchiv Preussischer Kulturbesitz (BPK), Berlin; front, Larry Burrows, courtesy Karachi Museum; Museum of Chinese History, photographed by Zhao Guangtian—©photo R.M.N-D. Arnaudet/G.Blot; art by Jerry Lofaro; BPK, Berlin.

All maps by John Drummond, Time Life Inc.

All icons by Maria DiLeo.

3: Scala, Florence. **4:** Gianni Dagli Orti, Paris—©photo R.M.N-H. Lewandoski. **5:** Art by John Rush—Corbis-Bettmann; Scala, Florence —©Erich Lessing. **6, 7:** Art by Nick Backes—Pierre Colombel, Paris—Anthony Bannister, NHPA, Ardingly, Sussex (insets); Coll. Musée de l'Homme, Cl. J. Oster (2)—©photo R.M.N. **8:** Jean Vertut, Paris—art by Maria DiLeo. **9:** Sisse Brimberg/National Geographic Society, Image Collection—Olga Soffer/ University of Illinois; art by Burt Silverman, background photograph from ENTHEOS—©Leonard Lee Rue III—George Chaloupka Collection. **10, 11:** Art by Fred Holz—©1998 Enrico Ferorelli; Robert Frerck/ Odyssey, Chicago; Ara Güler. **12:** ©Photo R.M.N-D. Arnaudet/G. Blot. **13:** Friedrich-Schiller-Universität Jena, Hilprecht-Sammlung, photo by Günther Schölitz; ©photo R.M.N-G. Blot—Giraudon/Art Resource, N.Y.; copyright the British Museum, London. **14:** Art by Maria DiLeo—Hirmer Fotoarchiv, Munich (2); copyright the British Museum, London. **15:** Art by Michael Jaroszko; art by Maria DiLeo—Charles & Josette Lenars/Corbis— copyright the British Museum, London. **16:** ©AKG Photo, Berlin/Iraq Museum, Baghdad, photo by Erich Lessing—Powerstock/Zefa, London— AKG Photo, Berlin/Paris, Musée du Louvre, photo by Erich Lessing; Eberhard Thiem, Lotus Film, Kaufbeuren/Iraq Museum, Baghdad, 1990. **17:** Dean Conger/Corbis; art by Fred Holz (inset)—courtesy Oriental Institute of the University of Chicago. **18:** Michael Freeman, courtesy Ashmolean Museum, Oxford, England—art by Frederic F. Bigio from B-C Graphics, based on information supplied by I. L. Finkel, London, ©1987 Time-Life Books—art by Michael Jaroszko; Erwin Böhm, Mainz. **19:** Art by Nick Backes; copyright the British Museum, London—From *Minds on Math*, ©1996 Addison-Wesley, Robert Moss Photography, Alexandria, Va. **20:** University of Pennsylvania Museum, neg. no. T35-110; the University Museum, University of Pennsylvania, photographed by Robert Lautman. **21:** Iraq Museum, Baghdad/Scala, Florence; copyright the British Museum, London (2)—University of Pennsylvania Museum, neg. no. T4-28c.3; *Illustrated London News* Picture Library, London. **22:** Claus Hansmann, Munich/Iraq Museum, Baghdad—Hirmer Fotoarchiv, Munich. **23:** Staatliche Museen zu Berlin-Preussischer Kulturbesitz, Vorderasiatisches Museum, photo by Jürgen Liepe (2); the British Library, London—Jean Loup Charmet, Paris. **24, 25:** ©Erich Lessing—Jacques Livet, Paris; Guido Alberto Rossi, Milan—Claus Hansmann, Munich/Egyptian Museum, Cairo; ©Barry Iverson; Gianni Dagli Orti, Paris; ©Jürgen Liepe, Berlin/ Egyptian Museum, Cairo; Lee Boltin Photo Library—©Erich Lessing; Walter Sanders for *Life*. **26, 27:** A. Ponzio/Shapowalow, Hamburg; Klaus-D. Francke/Bilderberg, Hamburg; ©Barry Iverson—Rudolf Gantenbrink, Munich; art by Fred Holz (inset); art by Laura Stutzman, Eloqui Inc., ©1996 Time-Life Books; Jean-Loup Charmet, Paris. **28:** Gianni Dagli Orti, Paris—Eberhard Thiem/Lotus Film, Kaufbeuren; Heaton/Shapowalow,

Hamburg—AKG Photo, Berlin/Erich Lessing. **29:** Gianni Dagli Orti, Paris (5)—AKG Photo, Berlin/Erich Lessing, Egyptian Museum, Cairo; copyright the British Museum, London. **30:** Michael Holford, Loughton, Essex—copyright the British Museum, London; art by Michael Jaroszko. **31:** ©Barry Iverson—©Erich Lessing—©Barry Iverson; Mike Pattisall (paper)—Ganet, MCR/Gamma. **32:** Eberhard Thiem/Lotus Film, Kaufbeuren—Robert Harding Picture Library, London; ©Fred J. Maroon/Photo Researchers. **33:** ©Erich Lessing; Lee Boltin Photo Library (inset)—©Jürgen Liepe, Berlin/Egyptian Museum, Cairo; Robert Harding Picture Library, London; Laenderpress, Mainz. **34, 35:** Francis Dzikowski, Theban Mapping Project; art by Joe Lertola for *Time*—Barry Iverson; David Wallace/BBC. **36:** Copyright the British Museum, London—Eberhard Thiem/Lotus Film, Kaufbeuren; ©Jacques Brun, Explorer, Paris. **37:** Eberhard Thiem/Lotus Film, Kaufbeuren; Jean-Claude Golvin (inset)—Eberhard Thiem/Lotus Film, Kaufbeuren; Gianni Dagli Orti, Paris. **38:** Courtesy Getty Conservation Institute, Los Angeles, U.S.A., ©1992 J. Paul Getty Trust—John G. Ross; art by John Drummond. **39:** The British Museum, London/Werner Forman Archive, London—art by Dina A. Faltings redrawn by John Drummond—copyright the British Museum, London (2); Jürgen Liepe, Berlin/Egyptian Museum, Cairo. **40:** Courtesy Getty Conservation Institute, Los Angeles, U.S.A., ©1992 J. Paul Getty Trust—©photo R.M.N-H. Lewandowski; papyrus courtesy Maria DiLeo. **41:** Courtesy Getty Conservation Institute, Los Angeles, U.S.A., ©1992 J. Paul Getty Trust; art by John Drummond—Staatliche Museen zu Berlin-Preussischer Kulturbesitz, Egyptian Museum, Cairo, photo by Gerhard Murza. **42:** Art by Maria DiLeo—©Jürgen Liepe, Berlin/Egyptian Museum, Cairo. **43:** Dr. Georg Gerster; art by Lana Rigsby, Lowell Williams Design, Inc., based on an illustration by Walter B. Emery, ©1987 Time Life Inc.—©Michael Holford, Loughton, Essex. **44:** Timothy Kendall; University of Pennsylvania Museum, neg. no. T4-543c.2. **45:** C. Sappa/Rapho—Staatliche Museen zu Berlin-Preussischer Kulturbesitz, Ägyptisches Museum, photo by M. Büsing; University of Pennsylvania Museum, neg. no. T4-550 c.2. **46, 47:** James L. Stanfield/ National Geographic Society, Image Collection; Larry Burrows, courtesy Karachi Museum—©C. Jarrige; Morihiro Oki; art by Fred Holz; Larry Burrows, courtesy Karachi Museum (4). **48:** ©Photo R.M.N-H. Lewandowski—©Remy Benali/Gamma Liaison; Angelo Hornak/Corbis. **49:** John P. Henebry Jr.—art by Fred Holz (4); ©1972 Marilyn Silverstone/ Magnum Photos, Inc. **50:** Madras Museum; Eberhard Thiem, Lotus Film, Kaufbeuren. **51:** Courtesy frankly.com; Frank Borges LLosa/ ©frankly.com—Ric Ergenbright Photography. **52:** Jean-Louis Nou— Clive Friend, Cobham, Surrey; courtesy Vilasini Balakrishnan. **53:** Michael Holford, Loughton, Essex; Benoy K. Behl—art by John Drummond; Xavier Zimbardo. **54:** James Burke, Time Life Picture Agency, ©1972 Time Incorporated, courtesy Institute of History and Philology, Academia Sinica, Taiwan—art by John Wang; courtesy Institute of History and Philology, Academia Sinica, Taiwan; James Burke, courtesy Academia Sinica, Taiwan. **55:** Denman Waldo Ross Collection, courtesy Museum of Fine Arts, Boston —Cultural Relics Publishing House, Beijing. **56:** Bibliothèque Nationale de France (2)—©Lowell Georgia/Photo Researchers, Inc. (2); National Palace Museum, Republic of China. **57:** Robert Moss Photography, Alexandria, Va.; insets courtesy Institute of History and Philology, Academia Sinica, Taiwan—art by John Wang. **58, 59:** Telegraph Colour Library, London; JPL, photo no. P-46827— Telegraph Colour Library, London—Bibliothèque Nationale de France.

Glossary of Terms

Abstract (**ab**–strakt) Designs that do not represent real shapes.

Acupuncture (**ak**–yoo–**puhngk**–chur) Traditional Chinese medicine that involves sticking thin needles into specific parts of the body to relieve pain and cure diseases.

AD (**ay dee**) An abbreviation for the latin phrase anno Domini, meaning "in the year of the Lord." It refers to dates that fell after Christ's birth.

Analysis (uh–**nal**–uh–siss) Separation of something into parts; to study carefully.

Ancestors (**an**–sess–turs) Distant relatives, usually living far in the past.

Aqueduct (**ak**-wi-dukt) A system of pipes and channels made of stone with a cement lining that carried water from distant water sources to Roman towns and cities.

Archaeologist (ar–kee–**ol**–uh–jist) A person who uses a variety of techniques to study the remains of past human lives and cultures by excavating buried settlements and graves.

Archetype (**ar**–kuh–tipe) The original model of something, on which all later models are based.

Aristocrat (uh–**riss**–tuh–krat) A member of the wealthy upper class in a society.

Artifact (**ar**–tuh–fakt) An object, such as a tool or pot, produced by a human.

Artisan (**ar**–tuh–zuhn) A person skilled in a paticular craft, such as a potter, a weaver, or a metalworker.

Autonomy (aw–**ton**–uh–mee) Self-government.

BC (**bee see**) Before Christ. It refers to dates that fell before the birth of Jesus Christ.

Cache (**kash**) A collection of items, such as a treasure, in a hiding place.

Cartouche (kar–**toosh**) The oval that enclosed the hieroglyphic name of a pharaoh, representing a magic rope that would protect him or her from harm.

Caste (**kast**) One of the four major classes in Indian society.

Catacombs (**kat**–uh–kohms) A group of connected underground rooms that were used for burial and worship by early Christians during the Roman Empire.

Cataract (**kat**–uh–rakt) Steep, swiftly moving rapids in a river, such as the Nile.

Century (**sen**–chuh–ree) (pl. **centuries**) (**sen**–chuh–rees) A period of 100 years, counted forward or backward from the birth of Jesus Christ. The first century BC refers to 99-1 BC; the second century BC spans 199-100 BC. In AD, or years after Christ's birth, the first century AD spans AD 1-99, and the second century AD100-199.

Christian era (**kriss**–chuhn **ihr**–uh) The period of time beginning after Christ's birth, from which we date all later events.

City-state (**sit**–ee–**state**) A self-governing unit made up of a town and its surrounding farmland.

Civilization (siv–i–luh–**zay**–shuhn) The way of life of a people who have achieved a relatively high level of cultural and political development, including producing a surplus of food, keeping written records, and forming a government.

Compass (**kuhm**–puhss) An instrument that shows direction by pointing to magnetic north.

Cyclops (**sye**–klops) In Greek mythology, a race of giants who possessed great strength and were distinguished by a single eye in the middle of their forehead.

Decayed (dee–**kayd**) Decomposed, or rotten, to the point of almost falling apart.

Diplomacy (di–**ploh**–muh–see) The practice by government officials of negotiating between nations.

Domesticate (doh–**mess**–tuh–kate) To tame or train an animal to live with or be useful to humans.

Dynasty (**dye**–nuh–stee) A series of kings or rulers who belong to the same family.

Egyptologist (ee–jip–**tol**–uh–jist) A person who studies the language, culture, religion, and archaeology of ancient Egypt.

Empire (**em**–pire) A nation or group of countries governed by a supreme ruler, called an emperor.

Epic (**ep**–ik) A long poem about the deeds of ancient heroes.

Excavate (**ek**–skuh–vate) To uncover a buried archaeological site by carefully removing layers of dirt and debris.

Exodus (**ek**–suh–duhss) In the Bible, the mass departure of Jews from Egypt led by Moses.

Fossil (**foss**–uhl) The petrified remains of a plant or animal that lived long ago.

Fresco (**fress**–koh) A wall painting made on wet plaster.

Generation (jen–uh–**ray**–shuhn) A group of people who are born about the same time, usually within a 30-year period.

Gladiator (**glad**–ee–ay–tur) A man, usually a slave or a prisoner, who fought animals or other men in Roman arenas for sport.

Homo sapiens sapiens (**hoh**–moh **say**–pee–uhns **say**–pee–uhns) The species name for modern man.

Ice Age (**eyess aje**) A cold period in the earth's history when glaciers covered much of the earth.

Irrigation (ihr–uh–**gay**–shuhn) A way of supplying land with water, using streams, pipes, or ditches.

Kiln (**kiln**) Oven used for firing clay to make it into hardened pottery or bricks.

Labyrinth (**lab**–uh–rinth) A complicated, mazelike system of passageways from which it is difficult to escape.

Latin (**Lat**–uhn) The language of ancient Romans, also used to describe the inhabitants of ancient Rome.

Lyre (**lire**) An ancient stringed instrument that was strummed or plucked like a harp.

Magistrate (**maj**–uh–strate) A government official.

Meditation (med–i–**tay**–shuhn) In Buddhism, the practice of focusing one's thoughts in a contemplative way to gain enlightenment.

Melanesia (mel–uh–**nee**–zhuh) A stretch of islands in the southwest Pacific Ocean, including the Solomon Islands and Fiji, that runs between Southeast Asia and Australia.

Mercenary (mur–suh–nair–ee) Soldiers hired to fight for a country not their own.

Middle East (mid–uhl **eest**) The territory in southwest Asia west of Afghanistan, including Iran, Iraq, Turkey, Syria, Israel, Jordan, and Saudi Arabia.

Migration (mye–**gray**–shuhn) The movement of people from one region to settle in another.

Millet (**mil**–it) A cereal grass grown for its grain.

Minotaur (**min**–uh–tor) Mythical half man, half bull said to roam the labyrinth beneath the Palace of Knossos.

Monarch (**mon**–ark) Someone who rules supreme over a kingdom or state by hereditary right, usually for life.

Monotheism (mon–uh–**thee**–ism) Belief in one god.

Monsoon (mon–**soon**) Season of heavy rains in southern Asia that produces much flooding and most of the water for the region for the year.

Mosaic (moh–**zay**–ik) A picture made on a floor or flat surface by fitting together pieces of colored stones or tiles to make a design.

Mosque (**mosk**) A Muslim house of worship.

Nirvana (nur–**vah**–nuh) The highest state of reincarnation a Buddhist can achieve, when the soul is freed from pain and suffering.

Nomadic (noh–**mad**–ik) Traveling from place to place, following food sources and never establishing a permanent residence.

Obelisk (**ob**–uh–lisk) In ancient Egypt, a tall stone pillar with four flat sides and a pointed top, covered in hieroglyphs, erected to proclaim the power of a pharaoh.

Oracle (**or**–uh–kuhl) A prediction about the future.

Organic (or–**gan**–ik) Obtained from natural substances, such as animal or plant materials.

Papyrus (puh–**pye**–ruhss) A type of paper used by ancient Egyptians, Greeks, and Romans made from the papyrus plant.

Patrician (puh–**trish**–uhn) In Rome, a member of the wealthy upper class, an aristocrat.

Patron (**pay**–truhn) A protector god believed to watch over a particular trade, event, or city.

Pharaoh (**fair**–oh) The title that was given to rulers of ancient Egypt.

Phenomenon (fe–**nom**–uh–non) A naturally occurring event that in ancient times was difficult to explain scientifically, such as thunder or lightning.

Pictograph (**pik**–toh–graf) A picture representing a word or idea.

Plebeian (**plee**–bee–uhn) In Rome, a member of the lower class, a commoner.

Radiocarbon dating (ray–dee–oh–kar–bon **day**–ting) A method of determining the age of ancient organic materials by measuring the amount of carbon-14 isotopes in a sample and comparing that amount with the known rate of radioactive decay of carbon, giving an actual age of an artifact that is usually accurate to within 5 to 10 percent.

Reincarnation (ree–in–kar–**nay**–shuhn) The belief in the soul's rebirth after death in another living form.

Relief (ri–**leef**) A type of sculpture that is made on a flat surface, from which the characters are only partially emerging.

Renaissance (ren–uh–**sahnss**) A period lasting from about AD 1300 to 1500 in Europe that was marked by a revival of interest in ancient arts, literature, and science.

Republic (ri–**puhb**–lik) A nation that is ruled by a representative who has been elected by the people.

Sacrifice (**sak**–ruh–fisse) The religious act of offering a god something precious, such as food, wine, gifts, or a live animal.

Sarcophagus (sar–**kawf**–uh–guhss) In Egypt, a large stone coffin that usually held several smaller ones.

Satrap (**sa**–trap) A governor of one of Persia's 20 provinces.

Scarab (**skair**–uhb) A small charm in the shape of a beetle that was sacred to the ancient Egyptians, who believed that it ensured resurrection in the afterlife.

Scribe (**skribe**) A person who writes letters and documents and keeps records for a living.

Seven Wonders of the World Seven man-made structures that were selected by the Romans about 130 BC as the most impressive and awe-inspiring in the Greek and Roman world.

Shards (**shards**) Pieces of broken pottery.

Stele (**stee**–lee) A stone slab or pillar inscribed with writing.

Stibnite (**stib**–nite) A lead-gray-colored mineral that was used for eye makeup.

Stupa (**stoo**–puh) A Buddhist shrine, shaped as a dome and filled with earth.

Stylus (**stye**–luhss) A writing tool that was used for writing letters on a wax-covered tablet. One side had a pointed end to write with and the other end was blunt, for rubbing out mistakes.

Tablet (**tab**–lit) A flat piece of stone or clay, on which something is inscribed.

Thermoluminescence dating (thur–moh–loo–muh–**ness**–uhns **day**–ting) A method used for dating ancient pottery. Pottery that has been fired in a kiln releases stored energy in the form of light, or thermo-luminescence. Once the pot has cooled, the clay begins absorbing light again. When scientists heat a pot shard and measure the amount of thermoluminescence that it releases, they can determine how long it has been since the pot was fired.

Trident (**trye**–duhnt) A three-pronged spear held by the Greek god Poseidon.

Trireme (**trye**–reem) A Greek warship. It was rowed into battle by oarsmen and used to ram enemy ships.

Ziggurat (**zig**–uh–rat) A temple in ancient Babylon and Sumer, in the form of a terraced pyramid.

Index

Index

K

Kakadu National Park, Australia: rock painting, *9*
Karnak temple complex, Egypt, *37*
Khafre (pharaoh): pyramid, *26-27*
Khety (Egyptian scribe), 40
Khufu (pharaoh): pyramid, *26-27*
Kites: Chinese, 68
Kithara player: Greece, 89
Knossos, Crete: palace, *76-77*
Krishna (Hindu god), *53*
Kumma, Nubia: fort, *43*
!Kung bowman, *6*
KV5 (tomb), Egypt, *34-35*

L

Labyrinth design: coin with, *77*
Lagash, Sumeria: ruler, *12*
Lao Zi (founder of Daoism), 65
Latrines, public: Rome, *104*
Laws: Code of Hammurabi, *13;* Ten Commandments, *72*
Legions: Roman, *114-115*
Lehner, Mark, 27
Libraries: of Alexandria, *97;* at Ephesus, *117*
Lighthouse: Alexandria, *96*
Linear B (writing system), *79*
Lions, carved: Mycenae entrance, *79;* pillar top, Indian, *52*
Lute player: China, *68*
Lyre, bull's-head: details, *20*

M

Mahabharata (Indian epic poem): painting from, *53*
Mammoths, woolly: bones, shelter from, *9;* cave painting of, *8*
Maps: Alexander's empire, 96; migration, prehistoric, *8-9;* Roman Empire, *116-117;* star, Chinese, *63;* Sumerian, *13*
Marduk (god): symbols of, *23*
Markets and shops: Greek, *86;* Roman, *108;* Sumerian, *14*
Marriage. *See* Weddings
Martial arts: India, *48*
Masks: China, 54; Egypt, 30, 31, 33; Greece, 78, 93
Mathematics: Greek, *90;* Indian, *53;* Roman, *103;* Sumerian, *19*
Maurya, Chandragupta, 52
Mauryan empire, 52; carving, *52*

Mausoleum of Halicarnassus, Turkey, *94*
Medicine: Greek, 90; Roman, *109*
Menkaure (pharaoh), *24;* pyramid, *26-27*
Mentuhotep (pharaoh), *24*
Meroë, Nubia: artifacts, *45*
Mesopotamia. *See* Sumer
Metics: Greece, 87
Migration: human, *8-9*
Minoan civilization, *76-77*
Minotaur legend, 77
Mohenjo-Daro, Pakistan, *46-47*
Money: Greek, *77;* Indian, *52*
Monks and monasteries, Buddhist, *51;* wall painting, *53*
Moon god: Sumerian (Nanna), *16*
Mosaics: of Battle of Issus, *97;* Roman, *99, 104, 105, 108, 109, 116*
Moses (Hebrew leader), *72*
Mother goddesses: Hindu, *48;* Sumerian, *16*
Mud-brick structures: Çatal Hüyük, *10-11;* Greece, *88;* Harappa, *46;* Sumer, *15, 17*
Mummies, *30-31*
Mummy's curse, story of, 32
Murex snail, *71*
Musicians: Chinese, *68;* Greek, *89, 91;* Israelite, *75*
Muslims: holy place, *74*
Mycenaean civilization, *78-79*

N

Nanna (Sumerian god), *16*
Narmer (king of Egypt), *24*
Navigation aids: Chinese, *63;* Phoenician, *71*
Nebuchadnezzar (Babylonian king): Hanging Gardens, *23*
Necklace: Buddhist saint's, *53*
Nefertari (wife of Ramses II), *36, 38;* cartouche, *41*
Nero (Roman emperor), *98,* 112
New Year celebration: China, *69*
Nile River, Africa, *25;* forts on, *43;* irrigation methods, *24*
Nippur, Sumer: clay map of, *13*
North Africa: animal exports to Rome, *108;* Roman outpost, *116*
North Star: navigation by, *71*

Nubia and Nubians, *42-45;* Abu Simbel site, *36;* chest depicting, *33;* timeline, *118-119*
Numbers: Gupta, *53;* Roman, 103
Nut (Egyptian goddess), *28, 33*

O

Octopus design: Minoan jar, *77*
Olive pickers: Greece, *86*
Olympia, Greece: athletes, *92;* starting blocks, *93;* Zeus statue, *92*
Olympic Games, *92, 93*
Olympus, Mount, Greece, *82;* gods of, *82-83,* 106
Omphalos (stone), Delphi, *83*
Oracle bones: China, *56*
Osiris (Egyptian god), *28, 29, 33;* statue, tomb with, *34-35*
Ostrakon and ostracism, *84*
Oxcart: toy, Indus, *47*
Oxen: Romans', *108, 109*

P

Paidagogos (Greek servant), *91*
Paidotribes (teacher), *90, 91*
Palace: Knossos, Crete, *76-77*
Pantheon (temple), Rome, *113*
Paper: Chinese making of, *56*
Papyrus, *40,* 71; painting on, *39*
Parthenon (temple), Athens, *81*
Passover celebration, *73*
Patricians: Rome, *102*
Pericles (Greek leader), *81*
Persepolis, Persia: Grand Staircase, *95*
Persia, *94-95;* cliff carving, *18;* conquest of, *96, 97*
Pets: Egypt, *38*
Phalanx: Greek use of, *80*
Pharos (lighthouse), Alexandria, *96*
Philadelphia Art Museum, Pa., *85*
Philip (king of Macedon), 96
Phoenicians (people), *70-71*
Pictographs, *18, 40-41*
Plato (Greek philosopher), *91*
Play festivals: Greece, *93*
Plow: Roman use of, *109*
Poems, Indian: contests, *52;* epic, painting from, *53*
Poleis (Greek city-states), 80
Polestar: navigation by, *71*
Pompeii, Italy, *110-111;* road crossing, *112*

Pont du Gard aqueduct, France, *113*
Poseidon (Greek god), *82*
Pottery, *11;* dating of, 10; Indus, seals for, *47;* Meroë, *45;* Minoan, *77; ostrakon, 84*
Prehistoric people, *6-11*
Priests: Egyptian, *31, 36,* 44; Hindu, *49;* Sumerian, *16*
Ptolemies (Egyptian dynasty), 45; Cleopatra VII, *25;* Ptolemy I, library built by, *97*
Puabi (queen): grave goods, *21*
Pump, chain: Chinese, *62*
Pyramids, *26-27;* Nubia, *45*
Pythagoras (mathematician), *90*

Q

Qin dynasty. *See* First Emperor of Qin
Qu Yuan: festival honoring, 68

R

Races: chariot, Roman, *106-107;* foot, *92, 93*
Radiocarbon dating, 10
Ramses II (pharaoh), *25;* mummy, *31;* sons' tomb, possible, *34-35;* temple, *36;* wife, *36, 38*
Raphael (painter): fresco, *91*
Rawlinson, Sir Henry, 18
Re (Egyptian god), *28*
Reed boat: seal depicting, *15*
Religion: Çatal Hüyük shrine, *10-11;* China, *64-65;* Christianity, 112; Egypt, *28-29, 36-37;* Greek gods, *82-83, 84,* 87, *92,* 106; India, *48-51, 53;* Indus, signs of, *46-47;* Jews and Judaism, *72-75;* Roman, *103, 106,* 113; Sumerian, *16-17*
Rhodes, Colossus of, Greece, *87*
Riddles: Greek, *89*
Ring, shield: Nubian, *45*
Roads: Roman, *112*
Robot explorer: in pyramid, *26*
Rock paintings, *6, 8, 9*
Roman numerals, 103
Roman Republic and Empire, *98-117;* army, *114-115;* banquets, *104,* 110; baths, *105;* building projects, *112-113;* children, *102, 103;* entertainment sites, *106-107;* gods, *103, 106,* 113; government, *100-101;* homes, *103, 104,* 110; map, *116-117;*

Time-Life Education, Inc. is a division of Time Life Inc.

TIME LIFE INC.

PRESIDENT and CEO: George Artandi
CHIEF OPERATING OFFICER: Mary Davis Holt

TIME-LIFE EDUCATION, INC.
PRESIDENT: Mary Davis Holt
MANAGING EDITOR: Mary J. Wright

Time-Life Student Library
ANCIENT CIVILIZATIONS

EDITOR: Karin Kinney

Associate Editor/Research and Writing: Lisa Krause
Picture Associate: Lisa Groseclose
Picture Coordinator: Daryl Beard

Designed by: Lori Cohen and Maria DiLeo, 3r1 Group

Special Contributors: Patricia Daniels, Jim Lynch (editing); Susan Perry (writing);
Jocelyn Lindsay, Donna M. Lucey, Terrell Smith (research and writing); Vilasini
Balakrishnan (research); Barbara Klein (index).
Senior Copyeditor: Judith Klein
Correspondents: Maria Vincenza Aloisi (Paris), Christine Hinze (London),
Christina Lieberman (New York).

Vice President of Marketing and Publisher: Rosalyn McPherson Andrews
Vice President of Sales: Robert F. Sheridan
Director of Book Production: Patricia Pascale
Director of Publishing Technology: Betsi McGrath
Director of Photography and Research: John Conrad Weiser
Marketing Manager: Michelle Stegmaier
Production Manager: Gertraude Schaefer
Quality Assurance Manager: James King
Chief Librarian: Louise D. Forstall
Direct Marketing Consultant: Barbara Erlandson

Consultants: Ben F. Collins was an ancient-world-history teacher at Surrattsville
High School in Prince Georges County, Md. For 32 years he explored with his
students the development and characteristics of world civilizations. He traveled
with his students throughout the eastern Mediterranean and was a *Washington
Post* Agnes Meyer Outstanding Teacher. He has worked as a history consultant
for the Discovery Channel and the Steck-Vaughn Company.

John McNeill is a professor of history at Georgetown University in Washington,
D.C. He specializes in world history, environmental history, and the history of
the Mediterranean basin.

First printing. Printed in U.S.A.
School and library distribution by Time-Life Education, P.O. Box 85026,
Richmond, Virginia 23285-5026.
Telephone: 1-800-449-2010
Internet: WWW.TIMELIFEEDU.COM

TIME-LIFE is a trademark of Time Warner Inc. U.S.A.

Library of Congress Cataloging-in-Publication Data
Ancient civilizations, 2500 BC-AD 500.
   p. cm. — (Time-Life student library)
   Includes index.
   Summary: Describes the people, culture, antiquities, and influences of ancient
civilizations, starting with early humans and moving chronologically through Sumer, Egypt,
Nubia, India, China, Israel, Greece, Rome, and others.
     ISBN 0-7835-1352-6
     1. Civilization, Ancient—Juvenile literature. [1. Civilization, Ancient. 2. Antiquities.]
I. Time-Life Books. II. Series.
CB311.A524 1998   98-22280
930—dc21   CIP
                                                  AC

OTHER PUBLICATIONS

TIME-LIFE KIDS
Library of First Questions and
   Answers
A Child's First Library of Learning
I Love Math
Nature Company Discoveries
Understanding Science & Nature

HISTORY
Our American Century
World War II
What Life Was Like
The American Story
Voices of the Civil War
The American Indians
Lost Civilizations
Mysteries of the Unknown
Time Frame
The Civil War
Cultural Atlas

SCIENCE/NATURE
Voyage Through the Universe

DO IT YOURSELF
Total Golf
How to Fix It
The Time-Life Complete Gardener
Home Repair and Improvement
The Art of Woodworking

COOKING
Weight Watchers® Smart Choice
   Recipe Collection
Great Taste-Low Fat
Williams-Sonoma Kitchen Library

For information on and a full description of any of the Time-Life Books series
listed above, please call 1-800-621-7026 or write:

Reader Information
Time-Life Customer Service
P.O. Box C-32068
Richmond, Virginia 23261-2068